The *Well-Adjusted Soul*™

FEEL-GOOD STORIES FROM THE HEART OF CHIROPRACTIC
VOLUME 1

This Gift of Health and Wellness Provided by:

Chiropractically Yours,
Dr. Mandy Jairell

D0980618

Aspen Family Chiropractic

If the book you are reading is not your own and you would like to purchase a copy for yourself or a friend, simply visit our online store at www.parkershareproducts.com/TWAS or call toll-free: 800-950-8044.

Dedication

This book is dedicated to all who have suffered and found peace in their recovery and to all who seek to discover the life-affirming joy of optimum health and wellness.

Patient Privacy Disclaimer

As a matter of professional ethics, it is the obligation of every chiropractor to protect the privacy of his or her patients. In many countries, this protection is a matter of civil law. Therefore, throughout this book, every effort has been made to address patient privacy concerns. Many patients whose stories are featured have readily agreed to have their real names used and have gone so far as to complete forms authorizing such use. Others have asked that they be identified with an alias to protect their own privacy and that of other members of their families. In still other cases, the events described happened so long ago that the doctor would find it nearly impossible to locate the patient and has simply utilized a patient pseudonym. For editorial reasons, no attempt will be made within individual stories to notify readers as to whether the names used are real or not. Of course, when references are made to celebrities, no name changes will have been introduced.

downtown monks

Albert Holtz osb

downtown monks

D0980613

sketches

of God

in the city

Albert Holtz, O.S.B.

illustrations by the author

ave maria press   Notre Dame, IN

To my brothers

at Newark Abbey

International Standard Book Number: 0-87793-696-X

Cover and text design by Brian C. Conley

Printed and bound in the United States of America.

Library of Congress Cataloging-in-Publication Data

Holtz, Albert.
    Downtown Monks : Sketches of God in the City/ Albert Holtz.
            p.   cm.
    Includes bibliographical references.
    ISBN 0-87793-696-X (pbk.)
    1. Christian Life—Catholic authors. 2. Benedictines—Spiritual life. 3. Christian life Anecdotes. 4. Benedictines—New Jersey—Newark Anecdotes.
I. Title.
BX2350.2.H5866   2000
271'.1074932—dc21

                                    (99-42616)
                                       CIP

Contents

Introduction

It's as good a place as any to look for God.

Begin in the very center of downtown Newark, New Jersey, at the intersection of Broad and Market, and walk west. Thread your way among mothers tugging toddlers, teenage boys in baggy jeans, and men and women in business suits shopping on their lunch hour. As you pass jewelry shops selling gold chains and the electronics stores with throbbing rap music, give a nod to the man whose shiny little lunch cart gives off a delicious aroma of sausage and shish kebab, a scent that mingles with the exhaust fumes of four lanes of buses and cars.

Move on past the clothing boutiques, the sneaker stores, and sidewalk displays of folding umbrellas, red nylon knapsacks, and woolen New York Giants caps. After two long, treeless blocks, you will see the furniture store with the big yellow sign *"Credito fácil y amistoso"* at the corner of Market and Washington.

Here the tall buildings suddenly end, the crowds thin out, and a wide view opens westward up a long slope. Let your eye wander uphill for three or four blocks, past the Burger King to the dignified gray pillars of the courthouse. Then follow the horizon off to the left until you see the red brick church tower standing straight and tall against the sky. That's us. Newark Abbey. To be more exact, that's the bell tower of St. Mary's, our abbey church, and next to it, hidden behind the buildings of St. Benedict's Preparatory School and St. Mary's Grammar School, is the monastery where we Benedictine monks have been working and praying since the 1850s.

This book tells of some of the ways we meet God there each day.

In his *Rule for Monks* (sometimes called simply *The Holy Rule*) St. Benedict says that the monastic task is to "seek God." At the heart of this search is a pair of remarkable assumptions: first, that God is present everywhere, and second, that Christ is to be met in every human being in the world. This book shows how a community of eighteen monks, relying on these two principles, have found downtown Newark a marvelous place to meet God.

Part One, "Searching Where You Are," is meant to be read first, since it sets the scene and gives background information for the rest of the book. Its five chapters are meditations on how a Benedictine meets God by living out the vow of stability in one particular place over a period of years. One important advantage of stability is that it allows you to reflect on the stories of a place and see how God has been acting there. The history of Newark Abbey is itself an extraordinary tale of God's working wonders in and through the lives of a small group of monks on a hill in the heart of New Jersey's largest city.

Part Two, "Searching in the Everyday," reminds us that all created reality is infused with the sacred, and that it is every Christian's pleasant task to uncover that presence every day in order to find—and be found by—God. The stories in this section celebrate how God comes to us in unexpected and often challenging ways.

Part Three, "Searching With the Neighbors," might seem a little surprising at first. With our two Ph.D's, a bunch of Masters degrees, and the hours we spend in meditation, reflection, and reading, you might expect that the Newark Benedictines, especially in a poor neighborhood such as ours, would be in the position of teaching the people who live around us. The stories in this part show, however, that over the years we have actually learned far more from our neighbors than they have from us—even such monastic virtues as trust in God, humility, and passionate response to the Lord's call.

Part Four, "Searching in Prayer," shows that genuine prayer does not draw us out of the world but helps us to see more deeply into it. This basic insight holds true for any believer's attempts to find intimacy with God, whether inside or outside the cloister. These five stories suggest that given the chance, whether in a liturgical service or in a silent prayer muttered in a classroom, God will often surprise us with some gift we never dreamed of.

Part Five, "Searching in the Common Life," speaks to all Christians who are called to seek and be found by God within the embrace of a family, an intimate friendship, or any other loving relationship. These five meditations on community living explore the connection between loving our brothers and sisters and our final destiny, union with God.

Part Six, "The End of the Journey," suggests some of the ways our lives can be enriched and deepened by a proper perspective on the world that is yet to come. The Christian life, and the monastic life in particular, must ultimately point beyond the present world to the Kingdom of Promise.

If you are someone who is seeking God in the seething center of a city—or in the constant commotion of a houseful of children—take heart in Benedict's two great insights: God is present everywhere, and you meet Christ in everyone. The stories in this book are especially for you. The Downtown Monks follow a way of life that is fifteen centuries old, but you may find it to be surprisingly like your own. We aren't called to live on a quiet mountaintop nor in a desert retreat. Like you, we seek and are sought by a loving God right where we are.

.

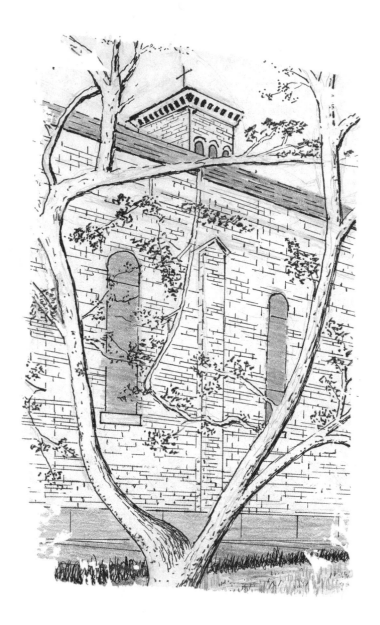

1

Searching Where You Are

STABILITY: FATHER CELESTINE

We may like to think of ourselves as people who are seeking God, but the Bible is very clear that it is really the other way around: it is God who is constantly seeking us. Every page of sacred scripture shows a God in love, a God ardently, passionately pursuing the human heart. From the biblical point of view, then, our main task is to let ourselves be caught and wrapped up in the Lord's loving embrace. Monastic spirituality expresses this in an apparent paradox: the quickest way to move ahead on the monastic quest is to stay in one place.

"Scratch hard enough around here, you know, and Benedictinism comes right up out of the ground." Fr. Celestine, who is ninety, drives his point home by playfully scraping his cane on the ground a few times with both hands as if he were using a hoe. A small man with wispy white hair and a slow, soft way of speaking, he has been a monk for almost sixty years. He was already a priest when he came to the monastery at the age of thirty, and was a big help in the abbey's parish apostolate because of his fluent German.

These days, one of us has to be with him whenever he walks outside. He stops after every ten steps, sometimes just to think, sometimes to say something to his companion. Lately he's taken to conversing half-aloud with the angels that keep him company.

We're out for a stroll on the grounds behind the monastery, and have stopped at the big white stone statue of St. Benedict on the new brick-paved plaza. Fr. Celestine looks around and takes in the scene. Down the hill, a few blocks to the east, the buildings of downtown Newark are stacked high against the blue sky. Nearer at hand are our two new playing fields, a running track, and a tennis court. There is a hint of mischief in his twinkling eyes as he looks at the fields. Maybe he's remembering the day, several years ago, when we were negotiating to buy those lots from the Newark Urban Development Authority. Although he was not a part of the negotiations, Fr. Celestine did his part to insure success by secretly burying Benedictine medals in the weeds. He seems delighted with the results.

Although the plaza on which we're walking was actually Shipman Street until 1975, for Fr. Celestine it—and the playing fields his medals helped us to acquire—are now as much our home as the older part of the monastery enclosure, built here in 1857. Back in the beginning, St. Mary's Priory was founded on High Street, on a hill overlooking the center of Newark. Gradually, over the decades, the city grew, spreading up the hill and on past, so that today the monastery finds itself in the middle of downtown.

Our neighbors were baffled, and some alumni and friends disappointed, when we didn't just do what everyone else was doing in 1972: pack up and move to a more promising location in the suburbs. But they didn't understand the Benedictine's sense of place.

From the earliest days in the desert of Egypt monastic men and women have had a sense of belonging to a particular locale. Many an old Benedictine has pointed out to the novices some trees planted when he or she was a novice, or an old building that hadn't even been built at that time. This is not just pleasant nostalgia; in the monastic tradition a sense of place is essential. Each Benedictine monastery is independent, so that we, unlike members of most religious orders, do not get transferred from one house to another, but remain in the place where we receive our first monastic training. Benedict assumes that ordinarily you will live in the same monastery your whole life.

Over the years, then, you set down roots in the place where you live and ties of affection, trust, and respect start to bind you to the others in the monastery, who are striving, as you are, to live the call as best they can. You draw strength from the elders' example of faithfulness and predictability, and the juniors' energy and enthusiasm. The place truly becomes "home."

We walk about eight steps and then Fr. Celestine stops, leans both hands on the top of his cane, and looks around again at the green fields alive with grammar school children running and shouting at recess. "God is good. Yes. Very good. Very good."

Geographical stability has a deeper dimension, however: it is the outward sign, the "sacrament," of being rooted in the Lord. Benedict knows there will be times when the task seems so hard that you will start to lose heart and may be tempted to give up the monastic life, thinking that God can be found better somewhere else. When these times of difficulty and confusion come, he writes, "the monk should say nothing and hold fast to patience in his heart, enduring all without growing weary or giving up. For scripture says: 'The one who endures to the end will be saved.'" The vow of stability makes you think twice: instead of just running away or transferring out of a painful situation, you go back and take another look, believing that God must be in there somewhere.

The saintly old monk takes a few more small steps and stops again, staring at a spot a few yards to his left. I know what's coming. He's about to say that there used to be a tavern right over there, and sometimes the police would have to come. . . .

"You know, there used to be a tavern back here on Shipman Street. That was years ago. Yes. Sometimes there'd be a fight and the police would have to come and break it up!" He chuckles at the humorous memories of the cobblestone street that once ran behind the monastery.

Our stability in the center of the city has a special message for our neighbors, whose lives are so often full of pessimism, weariness, and discouragement. When we stay where we are and try to be who we are called to be, we are saying to our brothers and sisters in the city, "You don't need to move elsewhere to find the Kingdom. Just keep looking right where you are: God is downtown!"

Too many times, though, I lose my nerve. I psychologically "move out" of the community or start searching elsewhere to fill up that inner void

that cries out for God. Instead of faithfully standing my ground when times get rough, I set off in
search of self-satisfaction by burying myself in
work or shallow distractions, or by manipulating
the people around me. Of course, none of these
escapes works for long, and by God's grace I
always find myself back once more on holy
ground, waiting patiently for the Lord.

Fr. Celestine starts shuffling again in his deliberate little steps, slowly enough to let the Lord
catch him. He is having one of those whispered
dialogues with someone I can't see. Probably an
angel who's been living in this very spot even
longer than he has.

Reading and Questions for Reflection

Read Genesis 28:10-19, the story of Jacob's
encounter with the Lord at Bethel. In verse 16,
Jacob says, "Truly the Lord is in this spot, though
I did not know it."

Take a moment to reflect on two or three of the
significant places in your life. How did the Divine
become present to you in each of them?

You may also be able to think of a place where
you have said, "God must be somewhere else,
because I can't feel the divine presence here!"
Take some time to revisit that place in your
mind's eye. Ask the Lord to show you how God
may have indeed been present there, too, even if
it was amidst the mystery of evil.

The Waymaker: Graduation

It usually takes a lot of patient looking and interpreting to see God at work in your life. On the other hand, every now and then the Waymaker goes public, working such wonders that no one can miss the point: this *has to be* the work of the Lord's "mighty hand and outstretched arm." Take for example the history of Newark Abbey since 1972.

It is Graduation Day, 1994. Several of the graduates suddenly jump to their feet singing and clapping in time to the music, as the school's Gospel Choir sings what has become our second alma mater:

> *We've come this far by faith,*
> *Leanin' on the Lord,*
> *Trustin' in his holy word.*
> *He's never failed me yet.*
> *That's why I'm singin', Oh . . .*
> *Can't turn around,*
> *We've come this far by faith . . .*

Soon all ninety-five members of the senior class are standing in their places in the front rows of the crowded auditorium. They're an unlikely mixture: most are African-American, some are European-American, and others are natives of Nigeria, Bolivia, or the Caribbean. A few take some tentative steps into the aisles, and before long the whole senior class has formed a spontaneous parade, clapping and singing their way up onto the stage. One after the other, Abbot Melvin, Fr. Edwin, and the other dignitaries disappear behind a wall of maroon caps and gowns.

The parents and guests, many of whom have been singing along with the choir, catch the spirit and rise to their feet. When the seniors have filled the last inch of space on the stage, the rest spill into the area on the floor in front of it, facing the audience. A soloist's voice booms out confidently:

> *Don't be discouraged when trouble enters*
> *   your life,*
> *for He will bear all your burdens*
> *and remove all misery and strife.*
> *That's why . . .*
> *We've come this far by faith,*
> *Leanin' on the Lord . . .*

Out in the crowd I notice an elderly gentleman waving to someone up on the stage. It's very possible that this will be the first of his grandchildren to go to college. A Portuguese couple crane their necks to see their son up on the stage. I know that they don't understand a single word of the song, but their smiles show that they're catching the enthusiasm just the same.

All of a sudden I'm at another graduation ceremony in this same auditorium twenty-two years ago. . . .

The young men of the class of 1972 are sitting quietly in the front few rows in their maroon caps and gowns. Almost all of them are white. We are all—graduates, faculty, and parents—somber and subdued, painfully aware that this will be the last class ever to graduate from St. Benedict's Prep. We are watching the 104-year-old school gasp out its last few breaths. For the past several years the flight to the suburbs and the general dissatisfaction with Catholic education have meant a declining enrollment. This, coupled with the lack of new vocations to the monastery, has caused the school to start losing money. The changing racial make-up of the city has begun bringing a new group of students to our doors, causing some disagreement among the monks as to how to deal with the challenge. This combination of problems has proven too much for the school. A few months ago the headmaster announced that St. Benedict's Prep would be closing its doors for good as of June.

Now the time has come. As Dean of Studies I am sitting on the stage, numb with shock and grief, presiding at the funeral. When I was a sophomore at St. Benedict's I decided that I wanted to become a Benedictine and spend my life working here; and now, three years after I started teaching, everything is finished: no dreams, no future. Waves of pain keep washing over me as I call out each senior's name. During the graduation speeches and a touching presentation from the senior class president of our rival school, Seton Hall Prep, I keep wishing the ceremony would just hurry up and end.

The soloist's voice snaps me back to the mid-nineties. Behind the rows just emptied by the seniors, the faculty members stand in their academic gowns and hoods: Benedictine monks and lay people, men and women, African-American, White and Latino, old and young, many of them alumni themselves. Some of them, too, are clapping in time to the music. Everyone seems to realize that something very special is happening here this evening. The voice booms from the speakers,

> *Just the other day I heard a man say*
> *That he didn't believe in God's Word.*
> *But I can truly say my God has made a way,*
> *He's never failed me yet . . .*

As the soloist sings "my God has made a way," the words send my memory back again across the twenty-two years. . . .

In that June of 1972, St. Benedict's Prep did indeed close its doors—presumably forever. Almost half of the monks moved to other monasteries right after graduation, leaving the rest of us wandering in a daze. That summer those of us who were left started having meetings twice a week to discuss everything from the role of an abbot and the kinds of work appropriate for monks, to how we could cut expenses—and what we should do next.

As the meetings continued into the fall, we looked at various possibilities for some sort of a common work, such as a retreat house or Newman chaplaincies. Right from the start, one option stood out above the rest. We had a trained faculty, completely equipped science labs, a fine library and an excellent auditorium, and most important, we had young men in our neighborhood who needed a quality education. So by

November we decided to open some sort of small high school for boys. On July 1, 1973, after months of planning and working and worrying, we began a school in the buildings of the former St. Benedict's Prep, with about ninety students (most of them minority kids from the city), twelve monks, one lay teacher, and not a clue as to how we were going to survive.

Over the following months and years, however, God kept opening a way for us. Somehow, whenever there was a crucial choice to be made we wound up making the right one, whether in selecting a headmaster for a school that didn't exist yet, or electing a new abbot the day before the first September classes began. Our alumni started to give much-needed support, and, one by one, new benefactors stepped forward, with gifts now totaling millions of dollars. Lay men and women have come to join us on the faculty, some for a year or two, and others for decades of loving service. Today we have well over five hundred students in grades seven through twelve.

In 1972 it was difficult to see how the Lord could possibly bring any good out of the tragic events that were changing our lives so drastically. Unable to see into the murky future, we had to operate on blind faith in God's goodness. The main lesson we learned over the next decades was probably this: the Waymaker specializes in hopeless situations. Now whenever our little community finds itself faced with a problem and there seems to be no way out, I remember the gloom and grief we shared in June of 1972 and figure, "Compared to what God brought us through back then, this problem's hardly worth worrying about."

The song ends in an uproar of cheering and applause. The sense of joy has spilled out into the lobby and probably down onto the sidewalk where even more folks are crowded around the front door hoping to get in. Over the past few years, the graduation ceremony at St. Benedict's Prep has become, like the school itself, a celebration of pride and hope for the people of our city.

The graduates and choir members file back to their seats. From down on the floor by the piano, where I've been helping with the choir, I return to my place on the stage. As I arrive back at my chair, the piano takes up the song again, and we all sing the chorus one last time: "We've come this far by faith, leaning on the Lord!" Filled with a sense of pride and thankfulness, I squint into the bright stage lights and pick out the faces of Fr. Boniface and Fr. Theodore, a couple of veteran faculty members. We have met God the Waymaker face-to-face, the One who searched us out in this monastery in the middle of Newark and keeps working wonders for us and through us "with mighty hand and outstretched arm."

My voice is one of the loudest:

> *He's never failed me yet.*
> *Oh! Can't turn around,*
> *We've come this far by faith!*

Reading and Questions for Reflection

Read Exodus 14:10-31, the account of the Israelites' escape from Egypt.

How have you experienced God as Waymaker in your life, whether in the distant past or recently? Did this experience change you? If so, how?

Where are you right now in your own salvation history? In the bondage of Egypt? In a time of wandering in the Wilderness? Perhaps you're feeling the exhilaration of being delivered from some danger or captivity. Take a moment to bring these reflections to God in prayer.

Hospitality:
First Day of School

"My name is Arthur.[1] I live in Newark, New Jersey," begins a small, quiet youngster. The boy next to him looks to make sure Arthur is finished, and then introduces himself in a confident voice:

"I'm Reggie. I like basketball and girls. I come from East Orange."

I smile. I lived in East Orange myself when I was a student here.

It's July 2, 1973. We're going around the English classroom introducing ourselves on the first day of school.

Educating young people has always been part of the Benedictine monastic tradition of hospitality. For years I used to say to my students on the first day of classes, "I live here. My brother monks and I have invited you into our home. So remember that, and please don't throw your candy wrappers on the floor."

I couldn't say it last year, because our school was closed. We've spent the past thirteen months praying, searching our hearts, and finally planning a new, smaller school. Yesterday we had a

[1] The students and neighbors portrayed in this book are all real people, but their names have been changed.

ceremony in the auditorium to mark the re-opening of St. Benedict's Prep with eighty-seven students. This morning, school is in session once again, as if its pulse had skipped a beat for a year and then kept right on going, just as it's been since 1868. It feels wonderful!

Since the fourth century, monasteries have been welcoming Christ in the person of the wayfarer, the pilgrim, and the poor. Benedict devotes a whole chapter of his *Rule for Monks* to "The Reception of Guests." It begins this way:

> *All guests who present themselves are to be welcomed as Christ, for he himself will say: I was a stranger and you welcomed me. Proper honor must be shown to all, especially to those who share our faith, and to pilgrims.* (Ch. 53)

Teenage boys haven't really changed much, I say to myself, as I look at the twelve freshmen in front of me and remember the first day of my own freshman year at St. Benedict's. *These kids are probably as excited and scared as I was, wondering what to expect.* Suddenly I'm staring at Arthur's head in surprise, trying to figure out what I'm seeing. Then I realize that he has a ballpoint pen and a newly sharpened pencil poking out of his towering afro, ready for immediate use.

As I look into their faces, a doubt starts to form in my mind: most of these kids, after all, are African-American and from the city. They don't speak the way I do; they come from a whole different set of life experiences. *I don't know these kids at all,* I decide, *and I'm not sure how to deal with them. For example, shouldn't I tell that student over there to take his hat off? Or is that part of his culture? I don't want to impose my white cultural values on him, right?* I swallow uncomfortably, trying to make up my mind on that one. *This,* I realize with a jolt, *is going to be a new experience for me.* For the first time, hospitality has become a challenge, an exercise in risk-taking.

It's easy enough to welcome familiar people who look like me and who see the world the way I do. Knowing pretty much how they think and feel, I have always been able to greet guests with open arms. Now, however, I'm being challenged to be open and receptive to young men who are unfamiliar, *foreign.* All of a sudden I feel the deep inner meaning of hospitality, and it's starting to stretch me.

"My name is Michael. I like the New York Knicks. Oh—and food!" Everybody cracks up at this afterthought since Michael must weigh 240 pounds.

You don't get to pick and choose when and how and where you will meet God. You have to be ready to greet the Lord in everything and everyone, especially the new, the unexpected, the unsettling, and the alien. Benedict tells us to receive the stranger as we would Christ himself. He knows that hospitality as openness of heart and mind is essential to the Christian spiritual life: you have to be ready to receive Christ into your life even when he shows up in the unfamiliar, the foreigner, or the stranger. To put it another way, you can never hope to really meet God face to face if you deal only with the safe, consoling, familiar circle of your previous experience.

"My name Robert, and I'm what's happenin'!" He's the one wearing a hat.

"Robert," I say softly, "Please take your hat off in the classroom."

"Oh!" He immediately whips off the blue Mets cap and puts it in front of him on the desk. No problem. Maybe this won't be quite as bad as I think.

Christians are called to leave ourselves open to the working of the Spirit with no restrictions. In fact, both sacred scripture and human experience show that it is precisely in the new, the unsettling, and the spiritually challenging that we are most likely to find the God we seek.

I confess that I'm not one who thrives on newness, spontaneity, or excitement. If it were up to me, I'd rather meet the Divine inside the narrow, predictable realm of what I can control and understand. The monastic life would be a stable, reassuring routine, where God would be a familiar guest whose presence I could just take for granted. To be honest, after thirteen months of shattered dreams, sleepless nights, and blind leaps into the future, I could do without all this stretching stuff this morning, thank you!

The room is suddenly quiet. The students are all staring at me expectantly. It takes a moment before it registers: they're waiting for me to introduce myself. Here goes. . . .

"Well, I guess you know I'm Father Albert. I went to St. Benedict's myself back in the Middle Ages. I live here. My brother monks and I have invited you into our home. So remember that, and please don't throw your candy wrappers on the floor."

Reading and Questions for Reflection

Read Genesis 18:1-8, the story of the strange divine visitors to Abram's tent.

Is there a situation in your life right now that is challenging you to "stretch," to welcome a situation or person that is new, alien, or perhaps threatening? What makes it hard for you to stretch? Can you think of some possible benefits to yourself that God may have in mind by asking you to welcome this new experience?

Consider the practical ways in which God may be calling you to offer hospitality to those around you. Perhaps there are ways you could make your home available as a place of refreshment. Or maybe there are other ways you could offer a welcome to "strangers."

Getting It Right:
Brother Denis

Today is the anniversary of the death of Br. Denis Robertson who died on this date in 1990 at the age of 80.

Br. Gereon, the table reader for the week, has just finished the day's chapter from the *Rule of St. Benedict*, and as I start eating my salad, he begins a commemoration from our community's necrology for today, December 20. He continues,

He was born in 1910, the youngest of eleven children. A fellow worker's faith so impressed him that he took instructions and became a Catholic in 1932. He entered the Abbey in September, 1934. Abbot Ernest's assessment of the lay brother candidate was: "He's too skinny—he'll never make it!" —which became more and more amusing with the passage of the decades.

I picture Br. Denis carrying a pile of test papers he has just mimeographed for someone, smiling his warm smile and greeting me with a cheerful "Hi!"

Punctuality, fidelity to monastic routine, and joyful service to others were his outstanding traits.

These were more than just his outstanding traits—they were the reason he could live such a joyful and peaceful life for eighty years.

An early riser, he would have coffee ready by 5:00 a.m. Then, after watering his plants, which were everywhere, he would sit in church before morning prayer, presenting to the Lord the long list of people he had promised to pray for. If something was lost, he would promise prayers to St. Anthony and would smile with delight upon learning that the Saint had come through once again.

He was, in fact, a close friend of the patron saint of lost articles, whom he sometimes referred to as "Tony." Never in a rush, he always had time for his plants, his prayers, and the people around him. Although he never took himself too seriously, Denis had a lot to teach us younger monks about seeking God: Br. Denis, you see, had it right. I remember the exact day when I discovered that he knew the secret of where to look for God. It was right after Christmas. . . .

It is December 28, 1972. St. Benedict's Prep has been closed for six months. The monks of Newark Abbey have decided to open some sort of a school using our now vacant facilities. We've come up here to "The Inn of the Spirit," an old Catskills hotel-turned-retreat-house in Yulan, New York, for three days to share our dreams and try to give some practical shape to our vague hopes for a school.

We're gathered in a circle in the sitting room of this old hotel. All but four or five of the monks are here. For two days now, in between walks in the wintry woods, we've been spending hours listening to one another's ideas and hopes for a new school. We've been working our way through our own homemade questionnaire, answering questions about our personal philosophy of teaching, our own strong and weak points, our hopes and dreams, and then sharing the answers out loud with the group.

We're on the question: "What is your theology of education?" It's my turn to read my answer. I clear my throat, to make sure everyone is listening. After all, I have just finished my Masters degree in Philosophy of Education at Columbia Teachers College, and this question gives me a chance to use what I've learned—and show off a little. I deliver a brief but dazzling discourse on the dignity of the individual and the school's duty to call out the God-given gifts in each student. After finishing, I lean back in the squeaky sofa, quite pleased with my eloquent answer and look around at my brothers. If anyone else is impressed they're not showing it. In the chair to my left is sixty-three-year-old Br. Denis. Now it's his turn.

"What's my theology of education?" He coughs self-consciously, shrugs, and looks down at his hands folded in his lap. The knuckles are all swollen with arthritis. Then he looks up and in a firm, gentle voice he says, "My theology of education? Well, I guess you just love the kids. That's about it, I suppose. You just love the kids." His jaw set firmly, he looks around quizzically at the rest of us through his thick glasses, as if wondering if there's some catch behind such an obvious question.

There is an awed silence in the circle as his answer sinks in. We all seem to realize that Br. Denis has got it right. I, the expert with the Masters degree, try to make myself smaller by shrinking into the cushions. He has just laid out for us in five words the guiding principle for everything we need to do from now on: "You just love the kids." Denis has taken Christ's command "Love one another," which is the principle by which he lives his own life, and has applied it to our non-existent school with a logic that is frighteningly simple.

I wish now that I had listened to him better. Over the next few years, preoccupied with the practical details of designing a curriculum and organizing the nuts and bolts of the school, I often lost sight of Denis' principle. I aimed instead for efficiency, for getting things done, not always appreciating the presence of Christ in the students who were all around me. I could quickly become irritable and cold with anyone whose needs or wants disrupted my efficient plans. But all that time, while I was so involved in what I thought was serious business, Br. Denis was quietly seeking and finding God in the *really* important things: cheering people up with a joke, caring lovingly for dozens of philodendrons and geraniums, sitting alone in church at 5:00 a.m. with his long list of names, and praying to "Tony" when something was lost. The whole time he still had it right.

I'm startled by a gentle tap on my left elbow. The reader has finished his account of Br. Denis' life, and Fr. Mark wants me to pass the butter.

Maybe Denis has been praying for me lately, because I think I may finally be starting to catch on. It's taken me a couple of decades and some difficult experiences of loving and grieving, but slowly I've discovered what Br. Denis knew all along: that loving is more important than "getting things done." I'm starting to see that when people "interrupt" my work they are giving me a surprise opportunity to meet Jesus and sit and listen to him, the way Martha's sister Mary did when he dropped in on them. All those urgent projects, those quizzes to be graded and deadlines to be met, seem less stressful when I see them as simply so many ways of using my gifts to "just love the kids."

"You just love the kids." Br. Denis had it right all along—and maybe I'm finally starting to get it right myself.

Reading and Questions for Reflection

Read Mark 10:46-52, the healing of the blind beggar. It's early morning on Palm Sunday. Jesus is setting out from Jericho toward Jerusalem, about twenty miles away, where he is going to suffer and die. As the procession to the Holy City gets under way, join the crowd. Feel the jostling. Smell the smells. Listen to the crowd noises, and hear what various people are shouting. Get into the atmosphere of excitement. All at once Jesus stands still and puts up his hand as if to say, "Wait! I thought I just heard something!" The great parade to Jerusalem grinds to a halt. Everyone seems confused. "What's happening? What is he doing?" people ask in hushed voices. "Why are we stopping?" You are wondering what Jesus could have heard to make him stop so suddenly. Then you hear it too, a feeble shout: "Jesus, Son of David, have pity on me!" It's some blind man. A couple of disciples have gone over to tell him to be quiet. A stranger beside you asks, "How could

Jesus hear that faint voice in the middle of all the shouting?" (Finish the scene.)

Is there some important job, occupation, or activity that keeps you so busy that you might not hear the voices of others in your life when they call to you for healing or help or simply for some attention?

THE PEACEABLE
KINGDOM: WILLIAM

"Well, we finally found out who's been getting into the gym locker room at night," Fr. Ed says as we walk down the hallway toward the cafeteria.

I shiver as I picture some shadowy stranger rooting around in our building in the middle of the night.

"Somebody's been stealing stuff?" I ask. I hadn't heard anything about it.

"No. But the maintenance guys were sure that somebody was getting in there at night. Nothing was missing, but there were little things out of place. You'll never guess who it was."

"Do I know him?"

"Sure!" he answers. "Remember William? A kid from last year? Tall guy, skinny?"

"Oh yeah! William! Had him in class." A quiet kid, but he'd had a rough time trying to get it together. One of the few students I've ever flunked, in fact. He had failed several subjects and so had decided to transfer to another school where he could graduate on time.

Fr. Ed starts answering my next question before I can ask it: "His family life is a disaster. Maybe you knew that already."

I didn't, but it doesn't surprise me.

"The last few weeks it got worse. His life just started coming apart and he had nowhere to turn. No real family to speak of. The only place he could think of where he felt safe after dark was here. So he started sneaking in at night to sleep on a bench in the locker room."

I try to imagine how it feels to be sixteen and to have no family to count on, no stable world around you. *But then,* I think, *we must be doing something right if William remembered this as a safe place, somewhere where he would feel okay, protected.* Maybe he got something out of his two years with us after all.

The big chain-link fence that runs around the edge of the Abbey's property is more than just protection. (And maybe not even very good protection: it didn't seem to stop William!) It also marks off the boundaries. It says, "This place is different. It's not like the rest of downtown. Strange things happen here: guys walk around in black gowns and hoods, get up at five o'clock in the morning to pray, work for no pay, and spend lots of time in prayer and silence." Definitely different—and strange, at least to the outside world's way of thinking.

For example, it's the date of your entry into the monastery that determines your rank in the community. The things that establish the pecking order in society—intelligence, ability, personality, social standing, wealth, and so on—don't count for much here. This flies in the face of the wisdom of the corporate world and the street, where

Darwin's rules of survival favor the strong and the smart.

There's a painting by the Quaker Edward Hicks called "Peaceable Kingdom" which shows an image from the prophecy of Isaiah, where a lion is lying down beside a lamb and a little child is playing with a snake. The monastery works at creating a "peaceable kingdom" where the mindless pursuits of power, prestige, and possessions are done away with and replaced by the single-minded search for God. This monastic ideal, which is really just the Christian ideal anyway, is what life, at its best, is actually about. This is what we human beings are made for: not for material accomplishments but for selfless, mutual love. It's what we are all searching for, whether we realize it or not, and it's where we're all heading in any case. The Peaceable Kingdom is supposed to be coming into existence in our hearts, our homes, and our schools, but it doesn't just happen. Like all Christians who pray, "Thy kingdom come," we have to work consciously at creating it all over again every day.

Monks live out this reality a little more explicitly than other Christians by our life of common ownership, humility, celibacy, and obedience. Our life can remind people that some day, when all the things the world values have passed away, there will be nothing left but love, the one thing that lasts.

We mark off a very real space in downtown Newark as a peaceable kingdom that includes a monastery, a parish church, a few school buildings, a garden, and some playing fields. Then we share the good news of the kingdom with others by inviting them inside the boundaries of our place. They come for lots of reasons—to celebrate a prayerful liturgy with us, to join the parish community, to be educated in our schools, to get a bag of canned goods, sometimes to join the monastic family by taking vows. It's far from perfect, of course. We have our share of sin and pain and ugliness, but we keep at the business of searching for God. The people who are drawn to the place manage, too, despite our imperfections, to meet and be touched by the Lord.

"I talked with him a while this morning," Fr. Ed continues. "It's really sad. The poor guy couldn't think of anywhere else to go, anybody to turn to."

In the Prologue of the *Holy Rule*, Benedict calls the monastery "a school of the Lord's service." Any school is, like the monastery, an artificial environment. It's not *supposed* to be like the rest of the world, but is meant to be a place apart. In the Peaceable Kingdom, unlike the larger culture, you take special care of the young, the elderly, the sick, and the weak. It is expected that all of us will make mistakes, and that we will use them to learn valuable lessons in humility and patience. Not surprisingly, some of Benedict's rules for the monastery also make good Christian educational philosophy. Take, for example, this maxim: "Let every attempt be made that the strong have things to strive for and the weak nothing to flee from."

To those who might object that the Kingdom inside our fence is "unreal," I suggest you talk to William. When the rest of his world was collapsing he remembered the feel of the Peaceable Kingdom and was drawn back to it because the love and genuine acceptance he'd found here were the most authentically human, life-giving, and "real" experiences he'd ever had.

We're at the door of the cafeteria. "Okay," I say to Fr. Ed, "See you later. Thanks for the news about William."

"Sure. See you around. Let me see what's going on in here." As the headmaster turns to step into the lunch room, I continue down the hallway. I have a French quiz to give in another part of the Kingdom.

Reading and Questions for Reflection

Read Isaiah 11:6-9, the prophet's vision of the "Peaceable Kingdom."

Reflect on the family or community in which you live. Think about the times when it is most "peaceable" and then the times when it is full of discord. Is there something you are willing and able to do to make that group more of a peaceable kingdom? Is there something you are unwilling to sacrifice in order to build a peaceable kingdom there?

2

Searching in the Everyday

THE GOD OF TODAY: CROW TALK

Never listen to crows; they can be a very bad influence.

The air in the cloister garden is cool and fresh. Since the sun has barely begun to lighten the eastern sky I decide to wait a few minutes before starting to read, so I lay my bible beside me on the bench and just enjoy the calm. Everything is quiet, except for the muted background whisper of distant cars and trucks. The reds and purples of Fr. Maynard's impatiens and the yellows and pinks of the roses are still gray in the semidarkness. In the far corner looms a twenty-foot sequoia, planted thirty years ago as a seedling. No one told the little tree that giant sequoias can't grow in downtown Newark, and it has taken root and grown lush and tall, proud. Talk about blooming where you're planted!

A raucous crow breaks the silence. I spot him five stories up on the edge of the monastery roof. When another crow answers him from the shadows, I smile knowingly. I've recently come to understand some of their language, thanks to one of my favorite saints.

A week ago I read a sermon by St. Caesarius of Arles, who died just about the time St. Benedict was born. In it the bishop says to his listeners, "Hear what the Lord says to you if you hope wrongly and procrastinate from day to day: 'Delay not to be converted to God.' You however, reply: tomorrow, tomorrow! O crow-like word!"

The Latin word for "tomorrow" is "*cras*," which sounds to Caesarius like a crow's call. He continues, "The raven sent out from the ark did not return, and has now grown old and says: *Cras! Cras!* It has a crow-like voice—a white head but a black heart. *Cras! Cras!* is the voice of the crow."

The bishop is referring to a verse in Genesis, chapter eight, "At the end of forty days Noah opened the hatch he had made in the ark, and he sent out a raven to see if the waters had lessened on the earth." That's the last we hear of the raven. Despite that fact that there was no place to land, it never came back, presumably because it kept telling itself, "*Cras!* I'll return tomorrow." But tomorrow never came. So Noah sent out a dove instead, which, as we all know, did return, and gave to the world the symbol of the olive branch. Caesarius concludes, "The raven did not return to the ark, the dove did. Therefore let the noise of the crow perish, let the sigh of the dove be present."

The doves that live in the sequoia tree are quiet this morning.

A second big crow swoops up and perches high on top of the school building. The two continue their loud plans,

"*Cras! Cras!* Tomorrow!"

"*Cras! Cras!*" agrees the other enthusiastically. The lively conversation goes back and forth.

"*Cras?*" asks the crow from his perch atop the monastery.

"*Cras!* Tomorrow things will be different!" answers the other.

A few devout Christians think like crows, always looking ahead to heaven, their gaze fixed on the next life, and never living in the present. They spend their todays getting ready for tomorrow. Others of us sound more like crows when we say things like, "After I've overcome this particular vice and get myself together, then I'll be ready to start praying." Or, "When I get that raise, then I won't be so stressed." Or, "Maybe next fall I can make time to go and help in the soup kitchen." The crow's call robs today of its meaning and lets us waste our lives in inaction and laziness.

We have other ways, too, of letting today slip by. It happens to me sometimes when I get too busy. You can't tell just by looking at me that I'm living outside of the present moment. For instance, if you saw me sitting in the monastery refectory during one of these attacks, you'd probably say that I'm eating breakfast. But I'm not really—most of me is already over in my office working on the first job of the day, a printout of students who received Fs on their report cards. Then I shift to the lesson plan I still have to do for class, and thirty seconds later I'm reminding myself to sign out a monastery car for this afternoon's meeting. Then I calculate what time I'll have to leave to get there by 3:30. At this point you'll notice me suddenly stare down at the now-empty bowl trying to remember what kind of cereal I've just eaten. I wasn't around to taste it. Too bad, too, because I've just blown an opportunity to meet the Lord. I could have been enjoying the flavor and the color of the cereal, or looking out at the morning sun bouncing off of the roses in the garden while I ate. Or I might have thought to give thanks that while lots of people in the city have to go hungry this morning, I've got something to eat.

Christian and non-Christian monastic traditions such as Zen Buddhism all agree that you need to stay in the present if you want to encounter the sacred. You can't really meet God— or anyone else—in the past, nor in the future, since both are beyond your grasp. The only time to meet God is now, in the present moment. This is why Benedict repeats those urgent exhortations from scripture such as, "Today if you hear his voice, harden not your heart!" and "Run while you have the light of day." This is the deep-down point of his insisting that we always be mindful of God's "presence," God's existence *in the present:* if I don't encounter God today, in the here and now, I never will.

The geraniums are starting to glow red. The sky is brightening with the light that announces the challenge of a new day.

The two crows, though, are already working out plans for tomorrow.

"*Cras?*" asks the one, just making sure.

"*Cras! Cras!*" agrees the other with gusto.

I pick up my bible and open it. Time to ignore the crows and start living in today.

Reading and Questions for Reflection

Read Psalm 95:7b-9: "Today, if you should hear his voice, harden not your heart." Sit quietly and listen for the Lord's voice. What is the Lord asking you to do *today*? What emotions does this request evoke in you?

Choose some simple chore such as washing the dishes or emptying the garbage. Try to do this task while being really present in it the whole time. Don't let your mind wander to anything else in the past or the future, but simply be present to this one task.

The God of the Real: Vibram Sole People

Some folks think that we live in the monastery in order to avoid facing the harsh "realities" of life, as if "reality" were an enemy of the spiritual life and might distract us from the lofty business of seeking God. That's not only bad monastic theology, it's not even Christianity. If you want to understand the true Christian attitude toward everyday reality, watch the Vibram sole people.

"Mostly what I remember is rain. It rained for, like, three days straight. And at Project U.S.E. you don't have tents." Project U.S.E. is a New Jersey-based educational organization that runs outdoor experiences like those of the more famous "Outward Bound" program. Sam is standing in front of the student body assembled in the school cafeteria. He and some of his classmates have just returned from a week-long hike in the woods of New Hampshire.

"So we just strung a big tarp between some trees and put our stuff under it, and cooked and slept there, too," he continues. There are sympathetic groans from the audience. As often happens with students involved in experiential education, it's hard to tell whether he's complaining or bragging.

The students are making presentations today about their Spring Projects. Every May we close up the classrooms and each student spends five weeks involved in some experience-based learning project. Some students have been putting on a children's play and presenting it in local grammar schools, others monitoring the e. coli bacteria level of the Passaic River and the lake in Branch Brook Park, and many have been volunteering full-time in schools and daycare centers.

"Learning by doing" means personal, firsthand involvement in activities that have real consequences. Make a math mistake when you're ordering the lumber for the stage set and you see the results very quickly. Help a retarded nine-year-old to read words for the first time and you change her life. Ignore the ban on keeping food in your tent while backpacking and a hungry bear barges in for a midnight snack. You're not *talking about* mathematics or *reading about* helping people or *thinking about* the need to follow instructions, but rather learning by really doing.

There are experiential education organizations dedicated to the principle that the best way to learn anything is by firsthand experience. My favorite among these are the professional outdoor educators, sometimes called "the Vibram sole crowd" after the hard rubber soles of their hiking boots.

"One day—I think it was Wednesday—we hiked through a swamp." A second Project U.S.E. student has now taken up the tale. "I don't know—I think we were lost or something. Anyway, we were in this swamp freezing to death when

Vince sprained his ankle. So we had to wrap his ankle. And Beth, who was one of our counselors, showed us this way you can lift people when they're hurt, and we had to carry him out."

There's something very genuine about Vibram sole people, something that rings true: they deal with reality as they find it. Every day they work in situations that challenge their endurance, their courage, and their creativity. They don't judge the "success" of an experience by whether or not it goes according to plan—the whole idea is to respond and react not to "the way it's supposed to be," but rather to what actually and truly is.

That is exactly what being a Christian is about, too: you deal with what really and truly is. The gospel calls us to find God not in theories or abstractions or pleasant pastel fantasies, but in the actual experiences and challenges of everyday living. Just as in outdoor education, chances are you may get pretty uncomfortable or even banged up a few times before the journey's over. A raccoon steals half of your food. You get lost. It rains for four days straight. Your canoe whacks against a rock and springs a leak. The search for God takes all of us through realities just as unpredictable and unpleasant, from misunderstandings and broken relationships to a telltale X-ray or a pink slip. The Lord assures us, in fact, that this reality is going to involve suffering: "Take up your cross and follow in my steps every day." This is the only way to live the Gospel, however: meeting reality head-on and letting the God of the Real meet you there. This is "Vibram sole Christianity."

"Anyway, after the rain stopped, things were pretty okay. We lit a fire and dried out our stuff.

And Vince had to keep his foot up. They took him to get it X-rayed next day."

Vibram sole Christians follow Christ by dealing with reality the way the experiential education instructors do: facing life's experiences honestly and, in the process, finding deeper truths about themselves and the world.

Anyone who comes to the monastery hoping to escape the challenges that life poses will stand out like a sore thumb. Before very long the would-be escapee discovers a frightening fact: in the monastery everything is arranged *precisely to help you to meet reality head-on.* It is a center for Vibram sole Christianity. The monastic ideal is to strip away all the falseness and let God work with the real you. The monastery offers no place to hide, whether in overwork or indolence, behind a pleasant face or a gruff personality. If you honestly accept the daily demands of community life and practice frequent introspective prayer, you'll be faced with larger doses of "reality" about yourself than most folks get in the "real world." And in the process you will be introduced to the Living and Almighty One, the God of the Real.

The whole school is applauding the hikers who have ended their presentation. As they file back to their seats, they each trade a "high five" with a senior named Rob. He's on his way up to the microphone to tell how he struggled for five weeks, working with an autistic five-year-old girl named Melanie. Definitely Vibram sole stuff!

Reading and Questions for Reflection
Read Psalm 29, where the psalmist meets God in the awesome power of the storm. As you read it slowly, bring to mind a particularly threatening

storm you have experienced. Let yourself feel the force of the wind and hear the crashing thunder as well as experience the feelings this evokes.

Where have you met God in an emotional or psychological "storm" in your life? Do you remember the feelings you experienced in the midst of it? Did these feelings change as the "storm" went on? Did the experience teach you anything about yourself? About God?

The God of Forgiveness:
The IBM Selectric

You bump into God at the strangest times. One of my most unforgettable encounters happened many years ago—right after I had done something truly stupid.

Two days previously, I asked Fr. Eugene if he would lend me his new electric typewriter so I could type a paper for a class in graduate school.

"Sure!" he says, happy to be of help. "Just take the whole thing, table and all. It's easier to move that way. Take the elevator though. Don't try to carry it on the stairs or you're liable to drop it." I agree readily and take the shiny new machine back to my office, where it does a beautiful job on my paper. . . .

Crash! The sickening racket echoes through the monastery's hallways as the brand new IBM typewriter smashes onto the first step. I stand frozen, mouth agape, holding an empty typewriter table and staring down wide-eyed at the pale blue machine that has just landed at my feet. I look up the steep flight of stairs and change my mind: there's no way I'll carry it up the stairs now! I decide to do what I should have done in the first place and take the elevator.

I set the typing table down at the foot of the staircase and glower accusingly at the front leg that caught on the bottom step and sent the typewriter flying. *How could I be so dumb? After what Fr. Eugene said to me, I still couldn't resist saving three minutes by carrying it up the stairs instead of going to the far end of the hallway and taking the school elevator. Now I've got this disaster on my hands.*

In a daze I bend over and lift the machine carefully back onto the table, coiling the long black power cord onto the top. I can't see any damage, but I've got a sick, foreboding feeling. I hurry, trying to disappear before curious heads start peering out of the monks' rooms that line the long hallway.

With the typewriter back on its stand I wheel it squeakily down the hall toward the elevator. I'm numb as I mechanically push it through the doorway and then onto the elevator. I poke the button with the "4" worn off of it.

Fr. Eugene was one of the first monks I had met as a freshman in high school. He was our music teacher and was in charge of the glee club. That's where I got to know him. I thought he was just the greatest. By the end of my sophomore year, I was convinced that what I wanted to do when I grew up was to come to St. Benedict's Prep and become a monk and be just like Fr. Eugene. Now, in my first year of teaching here with him, I've ruined his expensive new typewriter.

Fourth floor. I roll the table out of the elevator as fast as I dare—I want to get the next few minutes over with as quickly as possible. I let myself through the door leading into the monastery and squeak up to his door. I swallow hard and knock. I can hear my heart thumping.

"Come in, please."

I turn the knob and push the typewriter in ahead of me. "Hi, Fr. Eugene! I'm bringing your typewriter back."

"Oh! Finished already? Good for you!" he answers cheerfully.

I blurt out right away, "There's a little problem though. I dropped it. I dropped the typewriter." I hold my breath, waiting for the explosion, the scolding and the "Didn't I tell you to use the elevator?"

"Oh! Was that the crash I heard a minute ago?" he asks as if he were simply curious.

"Afraid so." I answer in a cracked voice. "I was starting to carry it up the stairs and it slid off and hit the floor." *How I wish I were somewhere else right now! Some place very far away.*

"Well, let's plug it in and see if it still works,'" he suggests matter-of-factly as he carefully marks his page, closes the book, and gets out of his chair.

I snatch the power cord a little too eagerly and, hands fumbling and shaking, I bend over and plug it into an outlet right by the door. *Please, God, please let it work! Let it be all right!* My knees are getting weak.

When he pushes the switch, I close my eyes and hold my breath. There's an odd humming sound. I half-open one eye and peek at the little steel ball with all the letters on it. He touches a key on the keyboard. The ball gives one sickly little twitch, and then the weird buzz gets louder. *It's shot!* He tries a few more keys, each time with the same result. *Oh, God! I've ruined it!* I start to sweat as I prepare once again for the scolding to start.

"Well, looks like something's broken, huh?" he says calmly, as he pops open the top of the machine and peers down casually at its innards.

"I . . . I'm sorry!" I blurt out, "What can I say? It was such a dumb thing to do! I feel awful." *I don't just feel stupid, I also feel as if I've betrayed his trust and let him down.* "Man! I just feel so. . . ."

"Hey!" he interrupts me in a gentle voice. Still bent over the ruined typewriter, he turns his head to look up at me. "Relax, please! So something's broken. It's still under warranty, and we can probably get it fixed for nothing. No big deal!"

I blink at him. I can't believe my ears. "You mean you're not mad at me?" I ask incredulously.

"What for?" he mumbles, his nose buried in the machine again. After a few more seconds he straightens up, gently closes the top of the machine, and adds, "These things happen. We'll all survive, I'm sure."

I'm at a loss for words. Although I still feel terrible, a new feeling starts to sweep over me—a wonderful sense of relief. *Look what I've done! Yet he's just brushing it off as if nothing happened!*

"Well . . ." I stammer, still trying to figure out this turn of events.

"I'll get Fr. Ben to call the service guy and get it fixed," he continues. "So do me a favor and don't worry about it!" His smile is utterly convincing. "Okay? Really. I mean it."

"Okay. Thanks a lot, Father!" I answer, forcing a smile. He's already walking back to his chair where he'd been reading when I came in. As far as he's concerned, the business is finished. But I'm still mortified and feel that I have to say something, anything. "Sorry! I mean, that was so dumb, you know?" I babble, "I just feel so, well, so. . . ."

At his chair he stops, turns back toward me, and with an amused look, gently interrupts me in mid-sentence: "Just close the door on your way out. See you at Vespers." He sits down, picks up his book, and opens to the bookmark.

"Okay," I babble. "And thanks!" I pull the door gently behind me until it clicks.

On my way back down the fateful staircase I start to realize the beautiful thing that has just happened to me. The feeling of being stupid is now completely washed away by the overwhelming experience of being forgiven. I'd stood there guilty and vulnerable and foolish, totally at his mercy, and Fr. Eugene simply let me off the hook! Not even a hint of blame in his voice or his body language. I've been completely and unconditionally forgiven!

The Lord has just used a kind brother and a broken typewriter to give me a glimpse of God's infinite, loving forgiveness. It's almost as if I've had a preview of the day when I'll appear before the throne of judgement, and now I know for sure how it will all turn out.

I'm almost laughing out loud by the time I get back to my room. I walk across to my cluttered desk. There, right on top of the pile of books, is my term paper, neatly typed on Fr. Eugene's new IBM Selectric.

Reading and Questions for Reflection
Read John 8:3-11, the story of the woman taken in adultery.

Do you find yourself withholding forgiveness from some individual or group? Bring that person or group to Jesus and ask him what you should do in this case. Can you offer to that person or group the same forgiving attitude that Jesus brought to the woman in the gospel story?

The God of Oneness:
Stokes State Forest

The trees are a jumble of black pen strokes against the snowy slopes of Stokes State Forest. Up above the ridge line ahead, the deep blue sky seems too pretty for December. The crisp air, scrubbed clean by yesterday's storm, is a treat for my city-dweller lungs. My breath shoots in short white puffs as I trudge toward the crest. The only sound is the steady, whispered crunch of six inches of new snow beneath my boots.

"Yeeeaiiiooow!" A heart-stopping scream careens across the ridge, shattering the icy silence into sharp splinters. It's Alan, one of the two eighth-graders hiking ten steps ahead of me. With a loud shout, he has just tossed himself like a sack of flour into the air and over a fallen tree trunk. The scream, like the throwing of his body, is for no particular reason. His buddy, Charles, somer-saults right behind and plops beside him in the deep snow drift.

I've invited them, two members of my Gospel Choir, to spend two days of Christmas vacation staying with Fr. Lucien and me in the monastery's house on our sixty-seven acres in the forested mountains of northern New Jersey.

In a second, they're out of the snow and off down the trail again, chattering to one another about some television show they saw last week.

The quiet closes around me once more. The crunch of my boots sets up its comforting rhythm again.

"This is so beautiful!" I sigh quietly to myself. The clean air, the pure snow, the quiet, the freedom of having nothing in particular to do until we go home tomorrow afternoon. Although my roots and my vow of stability call me to live in the center of Newark, the fresh air and the peacefulness this afternoon remind me of what I give up by living in the dust, fumes, and noise of the city. I come up once a month to visit the woods, hoping to bring some of its quiet wisdom home with me.

I stop to shake the heavy snow off a drooping pine branch, and watch it spring back eagerly toward the sky.

Benedictines, right from their beginning on Monte Cassino, have loved mountaintops. Up here it's easy to see the world as the sacrament of God, and watch the Creator's hand at work. On my long rambles, a few psalm verses come to mind over and over: "How great is your name, O Lord, our God, through all the earth!" "I lift up my eyes to the mountains, from where shall come my help. . . ." "Rocks and hills, bless the Lord!"

"Hey! What are these things?" Charles asks. The two of them are staring down at some animal tracks in the snow.

"Those are from a wild turkey," I answer. "Ever seen a wild turkey?"

"Only turkeys I ever seen are cooked ones!"

"Well, they're around in these woods," I assure them. "They're almost black. You may get to see one."

"Must be some frozen turkeys if they live out here, man!" Alan says. Then the two friends are off up the trail again, sneaking from rock to rock, moving on all fours so as to keep out of sight of some imaginary prey—probably a polar bear or a man-eating wild turkey

The snow underneath the tall pines is dotted with dark twigs and tiny cones. A set of rabbit tracks crosses the trail and disappears into the skeleton bushes. The great hunters are well ahead of me again, and the quiet closes in once more.

St. Benedict probably got his sense of the holiness and the wholeness of the universe from living in the mountains of Italy. He sees that the hills are filled with the glory of their creator. They are, therefore, sacred. He sees himself surrounded by the presence of God in hills, thorn bushes, ravens, and rainstorms. Then he takes this vision and expands it to include all of creation: everything in our daily human existence is holy, from the tools of the monastery (which are to be treated with the same reverence as vessels of the altar) to the guests (in whom Christ is received). Distinctions between the "spiritual" and the "material," then, make no sense, whether you're talking of trees or axe handles, mountains or cooking pots.

This blurring of any distinction between what is "holy" and what is "earthly" comes across in the way the various jobs in the monastery are described. The abbot, for example, who is the spiritual head and teacher of the monastery, also has the down-to-earth tasks of making sure the bell gets rung on time, assigning the daily work to the brethren, and keeping an inventory of the monastery's tools and clothing. The cellarer, on the other hand, who has the very practical charge of distributing to the monks all the various material necessities, is to do so with the same compassion and concern for everyone's spiritual well-being as the abbot: he should be "like a father to the whole community." "If any brother happens to make an unreasonable demand of him, he should not reject him with disdain and cause him distress, but reasonably and humbly deny the improper request." This monk who is in charge of the storeroom "must show every care and concern for the sick, children, guests, and the poor, knowing for certain that he will be held accountable for all of them on the day of judgement."

If jobs in the monastery aren't divided into purely "spiritual" and "secular," neither are the activities of the monk's day. You bring your meditation to the way you work, your holy reading to the way you treat your brothers and sisters, your tears to your praying, and so on. In Benedict's vision, praying, working, feeling, and thinking are all woven together into a seamless fabric. They are all part of the one most important task, the single-minded search for God.

"Can we go down there?" Alan asks. I've caught up with the two partners, who are looking longingly into a deep ravine that runs along the left side of the trail for the next half mile.

"Sure! Just take your time going down. And stay where I can see you."

They start sliding and jumping recklessly down the slippery hillside, at a speed that would make their mothers shudder. I shut my eyes and turn away quickly, leaving them in the hands of their guardian angels. . . .

Maybe what I'll bring back from the mountains this time is a deeper insight into the lesson Benedict learned from them—that God is present everywhere, and that life is a seamless whole, with no divisions between sacred and earthly. *Lectio* and lesson plans, housework and hymn singing, chapter meetings and common recreation are all part of the one quest—the search for God. Every Christian life has this same unity. Going to work, shopping, changing diapers, balancing the check-book, chatting with your spouse: all of these are sacred activities that lead us along our path to God.

Far below me, down among the rocks that poke out of the white blanket in the bottom of the ravine, the young hikers have now stopped and are staring upward. Alan is pointing to something in the top of a tall pine tree. Maybe they'll bring a little of the vision home from the woods, too.

Reading and Questions for Reflection

Read Psalm 8, which praises God as the maker of all.

Do you ever meet God the creator? If so, when and where are you most likely to do so?

Make it a priority today to take a few moments of quiet in your kitchen, office, or some other spot where you are usually busy. Just sit down, watch, and listen. Ask yourself, "How is God most present to me in this place? How is God a part of the work I do?"

THE GOD OF FAITHFULNESS:
THE DOGWOOD

A canopy of dogwood flowers floats over my head like a great white umbrella. The petals, glowing in the spring sunlight, pick up a tinge of pink from the red brick of the church on my left. Everything is quiet in this corner of the cloister garden—the noise of the evening rush hour doesn't reach here.

Underneath the dogwood is a good place to notice the steady, relentless passing of time. Two great cycles, the earth's four seasons and the Church's sacred calendar, intertwine in her arching branches.

At the start of each Lent, she sends out her first green buds, and then, around the feast of new life at Easter, these white flowers. When the petals blow onto the grass and turn brown on the path, it's time for Pentecost, for the breeze of the Holy Spirit to blow into our hearts. During Ordinary Time, just when the liturgical color changes from white to green, her branches will disappear under a lush blanket of summer leaves. Then, between the feast of the Holy Cross and the feast of St. Luke, her top leaves will start to turn a deep red-violet. That's the official start of autumn for me. Soon afterwards her boughs will run to shades of bruised purple, bright red, even lemon yellow. Then, with the rain and wind, come the final weeks of the liturgical year. As we, along with the rest of the Church, pray for all the faithful departed and meditate on the end of the world, she drops her dry leaves onto the lawn to scuttle and scratch across the slates. By the First Sunday of Advent she is in her winter sleep. Soon enough, after the long nights of the Christmas and Epiphany seasons, the cycle will start all over again. She'll wake up and send out her tiny green buds, as I've seen her do for thirty Lents now.

The evening Angelus starts ringing, marking off another period in the monastic day. I squint up at the bell tower through the veil of white petals bobbing in the spring breeze.

The Benedictine's life is one of cycles within cycles: the daily round—liturgical hours of prayer, community meals, work, recreation, and rest—repeats itself with comforting familiarity each day. The cycle of the week starts every Saturday evening at 5:00 with First Vespers of Sunday, the most important day of the week, and then circles around through the weekdays, remembering the Last Supper each Thursday, and the death of Jesus on Friday, returning to the Resurrection on Sunday, where the cycle starts all over again.

Strolling on the slates of the cloister walk to watch the seasons come and go, I realize that I find here a very special side of God. Not the powerful Waymaker who drowns Egyptian chariot drivers, nor the Unsettling One who challenges me to stretch and grow by shouting "Surprise!" as my plans go out the window. No, here in the garden I meet the God of Cycles and Seasons. This is the One whose steadfast love gives the dogwood her white flowers every spring and crowns her in purple glory every autumn without fail, the Lord of our days and weeks whose love makes the sun rise on us every morning.

For all the times that I stop and gaze up into the dogwood, for all the times I've delighted in the circles of days and weeks and seasons in the monastery, it's amazing how easily I forget that the God of the cycles who so faithfully watches over them is also the Faithful One who has loved me into being, sustains me at every moment, and who is always at my side watching over me. I get wrapped up in a project or a problem and become so focused on it that I start to feel overwhelmed. Maybe there's too much work and too little time, or some misunderstanding has left me angry and upset. Suddenly—and this has happened more times than I care to remember—the thought occurs to me, "No wonder I feel stressed! I haven't handed this over to God, who loves me so much." Sometimes I'll actually sit down and write out a list of the things that are bothering me, and then very deliberately hand them over, saying "Here, Lord, everything on this paper is now yours! Please just take all of this stuff and do whatever you want with it. I know you always come through." Every single time that I do this, I feel the weight drop off my shoulders and the knot in my stomach come untied. After a while I'll probably go and put my worries back on my own shoulders once more, and get myself all worked up again. Then, sooner or later, I'll notice the dogwood tree and remember the God of the seasons, and hand my problems over again. It's my own personal cycle, I guess.

I look up at the underside of the flowered umbrella as it curves down almost to the grass, and I stretch my arms lazily upward through the warm spring air. "Oh! That's right! I almost forgot! Lord, you know I've got this problem next Friday afternoon when I'm supposed to be in three places at once. You know that I got into this predicament by trying to be helpful to some people, the way you ask us to. Well, now I have no idea how I'm gonna get out of this one without someone feeling hurt! So this whole mess is all yours, Lord. Let me know what you come up with. Thanks!"

Having left the problem in competent hands under the dogwood, I turn and start slowly along the worn slate path toward the back door of the monastery. Another day has come and gone. Evening is here, and it's time for supper.

Reading and Questions for Reflections

Read Ecclesiastes 3:1-8, the famous passage that begins "To everything there is a season."

How many distinct "seasons" or time periods have there been in your life? How has the God of Faithfulness been present for you at each of those times? In what ways are you now able to see that presence better in looking back?

Think of one major concern or fear you have right now. Can you hand it over to the Lord in prayer, and let God worry about it? What would keep you from doing so?

3

Searching With the Neighbors

LETTING GO: WELFARE MOM

The majority of our students are African-American, most of them from the city. Perhaps twenty-five percent of them live below the government's official "poverty level." Although most of their parents edify us constantly with their example of deep faith in God and their willingness to sacrifice for their sons, one mother in particular proved to be a wonderful teacher to the monks. Her lesson is as fresh today as it was a dozen years ago. . . .

Fr. Edwin, the headmaster, hands me a note he has just gotten in the mail. Printed neatly with a felt pen on cheap blue paper, it reads simply:

> *Father Ed,*
> *I want to try to tithe my welfare check. I don't want my son to know. Your school has been good for both of us. Use this where it'll help.*
>
> *Sincerely,*
> *A mom.*

Enclosed with the note is twenty-seven dollars in cash.

She is a living example of what every Christian's quest for God is supposed to be: a series of constant "leaps of faith." True conversion can come only after you stop trying to be totally in control of your own destiny and give up trying make people and situations bend to your will.

The next month, after the welfare checks come out, a second note, this one on a sheet of loose-leaf, appears on the monastery bulletin board:

Dear Father Ed,
I'm putting this in the envelope before I lose my nerve. Talking about tithing is easy, doing it sure is another matter. I get scared when all there is left is faith and no money. Thanks for all you've done for my son and for all the kids at St. Benedict's.

A mom.

One sentence jumps off the page at me: "I get scared when all there is left is faith and no money." Suddenly it's 1972, and I'm sitting in the monastery recreation room. A community meeting is just ending. The heavy oak chairs are scraping loudly as everyone stands up and leaves the big oval table—everyone except me. I stay and rest my forehead on the cool tabletop and moan out loud, not knowing whether to laugh or cry. I turn my head slowly from side to side, mumbling to myself, "I can't believe we're going to do this. We've got to be crazy!" I'm not the risk-taking type. I've always prided myself on my logical, rational nature. But tonight, October 12, 1972, my reasonable side has taken a back seat. We have just voted unanimously to begin planning to open a school here next year despite some very ugly facts: We have very little money, but schools don't make money; they lose it. We have no one who has had any experience in administering a school. We are in an undesirable neighborhood. We have a shaky reputation since we closed St. Benedict's Prep just a few months ago. In the face of all these realities, however, we have just decided to take a leap and hope that God will catch us.

Over the years since that night in 1972 when we took the leap, God has indeed "caught us" over and over again. The school has a fine reputation for academics, sending graduates to excellent colleges, and its athletic programs are known throughout the state and even the nation. We have been able to buy urban renewal land and create playing fields next to the school, renovate the monastery, the abbey church, and three other buildings, and build a chapter room, a monks' health care facility, a gymnasium, and a library. Someone recently called St. Benedict's Prep "the jewel in Newark's crown."

That leap, however, is not a one-time effort but a way of life—not just for monks but for anyone seeking God. In the face of prosperity the temptation is to try to take back control from the Lord and start depending on our own efforts. To help keep us in shape, then, the Lord is always offering us new opportunities to trust, such as the lack of new vocations to the abbey—*"I get scared when all there is left is a successful school and no new monks!"*

The Lord keeps sending us a constant stream of marvelous role models, like that tithing welfare-mom, to remind us to keep relying on God rather than our own efforts. If we learn well, we can approach the future with the same trust that allowed the Waymaker to work miracles for us in 1972.

The next time the welfare checks come out I keep watching the bulletin board for a note from the tithing welfare mother, silently rooting for her, hoping she won't lose her nerve. Finally, a note appears on the board.

Dear Father Ed,
It was a little easier this time.

Enclosed with it—almost triumphantly, it seems—is twenty-seven dollars.

Reading and Questions for Reflection

Read Mark 12:41-44, the story of the widow who puts two coins in the temple treasury. Place yourself beside Jesus at the noisy entrance to the temple treasury. Crowds of pilgrims are surging in. As each one drops an offering into one of the trumpet-shaped receptacles, a priest calls out the amount of that person's offering. You notice the widow, stooped over with age, shuffling up to one of the boxes clutching something in her hand. "Two cents," announces the temple official. When you hear this, how does it make you feel? She had two coins, so why didn't she give one to God and keep the other to buy something to eat? Continue the meditation.

Reflect on the various kinds of "letting go" you've done in the past. Which experiences of letting go were voluntary? Which ones were beyond your control? Can you name one thing you'd like to let go of? What would it take for you to be able to do so?

GENEROSITY: MARITZA

God can make someone a great teacher at any age. Maritza, I remember, was only about four.

"Next, please." A voice calls through the little window that connects with the back room of the food pantry. A heavyset woman heaves herself to her feet and shuffles wearily up to the little window to get her groceries. "Remember, now, I got three kids!" she warns. Then she adds right away, "You got any meat?"

Thirty people are seated in five neat rows of folding chairs in the food pantry's crowded, low-ceilinged reception area waiting to be called up to the window to get a bag of groceries and, if they're lucky, maybe a small turkey for tomorrow's Thanksgiving dinner. Most are bundled up against the bitter cold that pours in every time someone comes through the door that opens out onto the sidewalk.

I notice a young woman has who just come in, standing in the back of the room with three little children. They all have her olive skin and dark eyes. Her thin coat tells me that she's probably only been up from South America for a few weeks. As I walk back to say hello, I try to imagine what it must be like to be poor, to have to scratch for everything, to ask for food to feed your babies.

We monks practice a certain frugal lifestyle, not owning anything ourselves, avoiding fancy material luxuries that could distract us from our spiritual goals. But this woman's kind of poverty is something else. It's grinding, discouraging, and deadening.

"*¿Dulces?*"

A tiny voice interrupts my thoughts. I look down at my right elbow into a little face that is turned up toward me expectantly. She repeats her request,

"*¿Dulces?*"

"Do you have any candy?" she wants to know. It's one of the three children. I burst out laughing, captivated by the wide, dark eyes and the billows of black curls.

"*¡Hola, chiquita!*" I greet her, and ask her her name, "*¿Como te llamas?*"

"*Maritza.*"

"*Encantado, Maritza.*" Pleased to meet you. I introduce myself, "*Me llamo Padre Alberto.*" Pointing to the tired looking woman next to her shepherding two younger boys, I ask "*¿Es tu mama?*" Is this your mommy? The young mother returns my smile and nods yes.

"*¿Dulces?*" The voice has moved around in front of me now.

"*Lo siento, niña,*" I'm sorry, Honey, but we don't have candy here, I explain. I picture the gray steel shelves in the back room lined with cans of lima beans and grapefruit sections, and cellophane bags of pasta and rice. No candy.

If Maritza is disappointed, she doesn't show it. She turns confidently on her heel and looks around the room until she spots the door that leads to Sr. Magdalene's office and the back room. Patrons of the food pantry are *never* allowed through that door—it's one of the few absolute rules Sr. Mag has. I wince as the four-year-old skips blithely toward the forbidden inner sanctum. Some curious heads turn to watch her disappear through the doorway.

Turning back to the mother and her two boys, I see that they can use more than just food. The littlest one is wearing sneakers with holes in the toes. As I approach the two toddlers, they hide bashfully behind their mother's skirt at first. I bend over, hands on knees, and make a few silly faces. They stare at me poker-faced.

Suddenly, looking past my shoulder, they start to smile and wave. I turn around to see Maritza standing in the forbidden doorway, smiling from ear to ear. She's holding her arms over her head like a champion who has just won an Olympic medal—and in each hand she's waving a hard candy wrapped in cellophane.

"¡*Dulces!*" she announces triumphantly. Not only has she returned from the inner sanctum alive and unscathed, but has actually come up with some candy! And not just one piece but two. I clap my hands a few times in appreciation of her success, and congratulate her, "¡*Bien hecho!*", "Well done!"

She scurries back past the rows of folding chairs, curls bouncing, leaving a trail of smiles behind her, rounds the last row, and comes right up to me. She stands there looking up at me, with one little hand stuck straight out in front of her. I stare down for a few seconds at the yellow sourball in her upturned palm. Then I realize that she's offering *me* one of her two pieces of precious candy! Her smile explains what's going on: she is so happy at her good luck that she wants to share it with a new friend she's just made. For her, it seems, this is just a natural response.

"*¡Gracias!*" I stammer, blushing and smiling uneasily. I want *her* to have the candy; I feel like telling her to put it in her pocket and save it for later. The obvious thing to do, though, is to just accept the gift gratefully. We each unwrap our candy and pop it in our mouths. I roll my eyes toward the ceiling in mock delight. "*¡Ay! ¡Que bueno!*" Maritza's face lights up. She's enjoying the sharing more than the taste of the candy. She couldn't be happier.

Maritza's delight this morning makes me think. There is clearly something deep down in us that loves to make others happy by giving. Maybe that's part of the image of God in each of us—the God of self-giving. This image can get quickly crusted over, though, in a consumer culture where what is prized is getting, not sharing. But this little girl has obviously been introduced to the God of giving somewhere. She must have seen somebody acting this way. I glance at her mother, and figure that she is probably Maritza's model of selfless generosity.

We each have opportunities to allow others to meet the God of Giving. It may be cheerfully spending ten minutes of our time with someone who needs our help, or using one of our talents as a gift for someone else's benefit. Or it may be contributing financially to some cause to the point where we actually feel the sacrifice. The generosity of good-hearted humans is one of God's favorite ways of coming into our lives.

"Did you get some candy?"

Sr. Mag has come over to say hello and fuss over the children. Maritza, baffled by the English, stares up at her silent and wide-eyed, her cheek showing a large, telltale bulge.

"Yes, she did," I answer for her.

"And what about her brothers?"

"Maritza," I whisper, *"vaya buscar dulces para tus hermanitos."* "Go get some candy for your little brothers."

She scampers off without a word, disappearing a second time through the forbidden door in pursuit of the God of Giving. Her day is made. So is mine.

Reading and Questions for Reflection

Read John 3:16: "God so loved the world that he gave his only Son, that whoever believes in him may not die, but have eternal life."

Has someone else's generous deed ever given you a glimpse of this God of infinite giving? In what ways has God been particularly generous to you?

THE POWER OF THE WORD: JOHN

The first time I met him, he was a rambunctious freshman, just out of eighth grade, full of fresh answers and wisecracks. John was the kind of kid that everybody in the school knows, the kind of kid who would need a lot of "straightening out."

It was the last day of school of his freshman year when John decided to play hooky, hopping on his bike instead of heading for school. A few blocks from his house, as he was riding across an intersection, he was struck by a van and flung through the air. The rescue squad delivered his shattered body to the hospital with barely a trace of life left in it.

Fr. Ed got the phone message. John was in critical condition and was not expected to live. When he got to the hospital, Fr. Ed found him in a deep coma. The doctors said the young victim wouldn't last very long, but when Fr. Ed returned the next morning, John was still hanging on.

Over the next days and weeks Fr. Ed continued to go faithfully to the hospital every day. Taking his cue from the nurses, he kept talking to his comatose student, sometimes joking, sometimes scolding, sometimes telling stories. There was never any response from the once-talkative freshman. But Fr. Ed kept on speaking to him anyway, hoping that his words would somehow reach John. Since he kept hanging on to life, the doctors now revised their prognosis: John would live, but would probably never regain consciousness. But still Fr. Ed kept visiting and kept talking.

Finally, after more weeks had passed, he returned to the monastery one afternoon with the news, "John wiggled a finger today. He's starting to respond!"

Soon after that I visited him in the hospital. He lay perfectly still, with his eyes closed. I gently lifted his right hand off the stiff white sheet and held it in mine. It felt alive, but in a strange way—it certainly wasn't the hand of someone who was asleep.

"John," I said, "This is Fr. Albert. You awake?"

He gave my hand one deliberate squeeze. One meant yes.

"You feeling okay today?" I continue.

Another single squeeze.

It was like talking to someone through a brick wall or through tons of rock after a mine cave-in. There was no voice, no facial expression, no words: nothing but a squeeze of the hand. Disconcerting at first, but gradually I got used to it.

We followed his progress all summer long. Finally, in September, three long months after his accident, John opened his eyes. Progress was still slow, but every day Fr. Ed kept visiting and talking. Then one day John actually started to speak! He would remain paralyzed from the waist down, but he had been pulled back out of the valley of the shadow of death, literally talked out of his coma by the power of people's loving words.

It's after school, and he is sitting in the school entrance lobby in his sturdy wheelchair, an island awash in the swirling stream of students, parents, salesmen, and poor people looking for canned goods. "John!" I say to the heavyset thirty-year-old bearded man, "What are you doing here? Looking for Fr. Ed?" The two of them still keep in close touch, so I figure that John—who has learned over the years to stand with the help of braces and two canes—has decided to stop by to visit his special friend.

"Sure I'm looking for Fr. Ed! Where is that man? He told me he'd be around, and now he's not here!"

In the monastic tradition, "the word" is tremendously important. The *Holy Rule* begins with the word, "Listen!" The monk's spiritual life is nourished by the Word of God both in *lectio divina* (holy reading) and in the public praying of the psalms and listening to readings from scripture or the spiritual masters.

On the other hand, Benedict, like most monastic fathers, warns that words can also cause problems. Wise people don't speak very much, he reminds his reader, adding that permission for a monk to speak should be given only rarely. One story from the lives of the earliest monks of Egypt gives a powerful if slightly tongue-in-cheek lesson on how deadly words can be:

> *One day a disciple of a well-known hermit did something wrong. The hermit got so upset that he said to the young man: "Go drop dead!" Instantly the disciple fell down dead.*

The hermit, filled with horror, started praying: "Lord Jesus Christ, I beg you to bring my disciple back to life and from now on I promise that I will be careful what I say." And the disciple was restored to life on the spot.

The lesson here is not just for monastics: any Christian would do well to respect the awesome power of words, and never speak hastily or in anger.

"Listen, I can't wait any more. You tell my man Fr. Ed that John was here." He wheels himself out the door to the top of the steep stone steps. He struggles to his feet, and, with the help of his braces and two canes, actually "walks" clumsily down the stairs to the street. As I watch him, I think about the miracles that we can do for one another with words. Do I really believe that my own words have that kind of power of life and death over the people around me? Can an angry comment when I'm in a bad mood really make a brother monk drop down dead? Can an offhand remark of mine in French class really be so momentous in some student's life? I look at John and think, a little uneasily, *Maybe.*

"Tell him to give me a call, okay?" John is hoisting himself into the passenger seat of a friend's car.

"Okay, will do!" I call down from the top of the big stone steps, "Have a good day!" Some teenagers passing on the sidewalk have stopped to stare at the cripple carefully sliding into the car. They don't know that they're looking at someone brought back from the grave by the power of the word.

Reading and Questions for Reflection

Read Luke 7:11-17, about Christ's raising to life the only son of the widow of Naim.

Has anyone ever called you to life through a loving word or deed? Recall the circumstances of when and where this happened, and how it made you feel. Is there someone in your life whom God expects you to call to life with a word?

Have you ever seen anyone deeply wounded by a word?

PASSION: GOSPEL SINGER

A slender woman about twenty-five years old steps out of the front row of the choir and up to the microphone. She looks around at the congregation, smiles for a brief moment, then, arms straight at her sides and fists clenched lightly, she closes her eyes and sings in a soft, passionate voice:

"I don't feel no way tired!"

I'm sitting in the fifth row of benches in a little Pentecostal church. The place must have been a store at one time, but a dropped ceiling, some red carpeting, and dark wood paneling have changed it into a church.

"I just can't believe he's brought me this far to leave me," she continues quietly, the electronic organ playing a hushed, pulsing background. The choir of ten women and four men in gray robes with blue yoked collars stands in two rows in the center of the sanctuary. They take a small step to the left, pause, step to the right, hesitate, and step back to the left again in time with the music.

Her hands are now spread open in front of her, palms up, as she pours out her troubles to the Lord. An elderly woman softly encourages her from the second pew, "Go ahead, now! That's all right!" As the soloist sings on with eyes closed and head tilted slightly back, others help her out with gentle words, "Yes, you just tell it!" "All right, then!" Others are whispering to themselves, "Jesus!" "Yes, Lord! Thank you, Lord!"

For the African-American community, "church" is very much about feelings. Emotion, far from being incidental to worship, is what allows your soul to be touched by God and moved by the Spirit.

You might expect that the *Rule of Benedict*, written by a sober sixth-century Roman, would be mistrustful of emotions and advise monks to avoid them. Surprisingly, however, the *Rule* is filled with emotional language, and expects the monk to feel things deeply. The monastic life is a search that demands constant energy and commitment. If it is not a passionate response to God's passionate call, then it is nothing.

"I just can't believe he's brought me this far just to leave me!" Now the choir joins in, repeating with her,

"I just can't believe He's brought me this far, I just can't believe He's brought me this far, I just can't believe He's brought me this far. . . ."

Benedict wants the newcomer to be enthusiastic about the monastic journey: "The concern must be whether the novice truly seeks God and whether he shows eagerness for the work of God, for obedience, and for trials." The Prologue to the *Rule* pulses with a sense of urgency, with images of running, while the final chapter speaks to those who are "hastening on to the perfection of monastic life" and "hastening toward your heavenly home."

A monk is to be "swift" in obeying, wanting to "arrive speedily" at the high summit of humility, to "hasten" at the sound of the bell to arrive before the others at the work of God.

"I just can't believe he's brought me this far; I just can't believe he's brought me this far. . . ." With each repetition the phrase has gotten a little louder, so that now the little church is starting to throb with the shout: *"I just can't believe he's brought me this far. . . ."*

A singer in her thirties taps a tambourine against her leg. She looks very ordinary, like the rest of the choir members—they are probably nurses, secretaries, bus drivers, and accountants. As they throw themselves into the gospel song, though, and their voices flood the low-ceilinged room, these very ordinary people are being transformed. The emotional intensity of their song is overpowering. I join the rhythmic clapping.

We are worshipping in a way that was born out of the African-Americans' experiences of slavery and suffering, of constant struggle and liberation. It speaks to the soul at the deepest emotional level. This is the kind of Sunday service that gives you the spiritual energy and strength to make it through the coming week.

Benedict expects the monastic to be passionate, a great lover of the other members of the community, of the superior, of Christ, and of God. He or she needs to be just as enthusiastic about fasting, avoiding vices, and overcoming temptations. The passion may be quiet, even reserved; the fire can be deep inside. But it must be there. Monastic men and women for centuries have passionately offered their talents and their energies, like the singers in front of me here, in praise of God. The great contributions of monasticism—from manu-script illumination, sacred music, and enamel work to architectural and agricultural innova-tions—are hardly the products of casual moon-lighting done just to kill time. They are all the fruits of a passionate love of the Creator and cre-ation. No matter what your work is, it will throb with divine energy if you do it wholeheartedly for the love of God.

"I just can't believe he's brought me this far, I just can't believe he's brought me this far, I just can't believe he's brought me this far. . . ."

People in the congregation begin standing up one by one in their places and clapping. Some lift their hands over their heads. I stand up, too, swaying and clapping, letting the music soak down deep inside me.

Listening to the choir praising God with such energy and feeling I ask myself, "Aren't all Christians supposed to bring some sort of fervor to their prayer?" Benedict talks about tears and compunction as a normal part of personal prayer, yet we often approach it with a certain casual-ness, emotional distance, and even distraction.

"I just can't believe he's brought me this far, I just can't believe he's brought me this far, I just can't believe he's brought me this far. . . ."

The choir is now holding the last note and the soloist is singing out a triumphant octave above everyone else. The congregation is applauding until our hands start to hurt. Finally the singers draw out the last phrase one final time . . .

". . . just . . . to . . . leave . . . me!"

Everyone in the place—the choir, the minister, the congregation—we're all on our feet, applaud-ing. The young woman steps slowly back to her place, drained.

The applause subsides, and we sit down. There are a few muttered exclamations of "Yes, Jesus!" and "Thank you, Lord!" as we wait quietly for the reading from scripture to begin. A silent prayer forms in my heart: *Lord, Give me this conviction, this passion. Make my life a song sung with this kind of abandon. Amen.*

Reading and Questions for Reflection

Read Mark 10:17-22, Jesus' encounter with the rich young man. In the gospel Christ is constantly challenging you, too, to follow him wholeheartedly and generously. Are there areas of your life that you are enthused and passionate about? If you were to respond to Christ more wholeheartedly, what changes might you have to make in your life?

Humility: Ice Man

The door that swings out onto the sidewalk jolts open and the icy wind shoves an old man into the empty waiting room of the food pantry. He's stooped over with the weight of seventy-some weary years.

"Good morning, sir!" I greet him, as I slide the bolt to lock the door behind him. "You just made it. We're closing up!" I get a rude shock when I shake his hand: it's like a piece of ice. "Gosh! Your hand is cold!" I say, "Where have you been?" I've never felt someone's skin that cold before.

"Walked all the way from Irvington Center. That's why I'm late." *That's four miles in the freezing wind,* I say to myself.

"Well, it's closing time," I warn, "and they tell me that we've run out of food." A shadow of panic passes over his face but is gone as quickly as it came. I try to soften the blow by adding cheerfully, "But let's see if Sister can find something for you." As he shuffles beside me across the red tiles of the waiting room, he carries himself with calm dignity.

The thought flashes through my mind that this old gentleman is completely dependent on others. Everything he has he receives from either the welfare system, a religious charity, or maybe an occasional friend or neighbor. As we get to the office door I call out,

"Sr. Magdalene? You still here?"

"Yes? Who's that? Fr. Albert?" A voice comes from the back room.

"Yes, sister. There's a gentleman who just arrived as I was locking the door. Do you think you can find something to give him?" By this time Sr. Mag has come out of the back room to see for herself. Despite what her gray hair and her mature years might suggest, she's a fountain of boundless energy, especially when it comes to "her" poor people.

"Well, good morning. My, you look cold!" she says in a soothing voice. She turns to me, "Thanks, Fr. Albert. I'll see what we can do." Turning back to the visitor she asks, "What's your name?" I leave the two of them in the office and go back out into the waiting room.

I start thinking that in one way the monks of Newark Abbey have something in common with this poor gentleman: we depend for our survival, the way he does, on gifts from other people. Over the years God has kept sending us generous helpers—individuals, corporations, and foundations—so we can pay our bills and serve people through our apostolate. We know that we will always be in a position of financial dependence on others.

This kind of dependency should have a familiar ring to it for a community of Benedictines. For St. Benedict, the central monastic virtue is humility, recognizing and facing the reality of our situation before the Almighty. The truth is that *everything is a gift from the Lord.* There is no reason, then, to get puffed up about our talents, virtues, or accomplishments—in fact, they ought to make us feel humble in the face of God's goodness to us. The gifts that people keep showering on our monastery give us plenty of cause for humility.

"Have a good day, now," Sr. Magdalene is saying good-bye to our visitor.

"Thank you, Sister," he says, shaking her hand, "Thank you. God bless you."

The gentleman is standing in front of me holding a large plastic bag full of groceries that Sr. Mag has conjured up from somewhere. She always manages to come up with something for a needy person.

"Well," I say as I walk him over toward the door, "I see that you got some groceries after all. That's wonderful!" He stops, turns to look me in the eye, and says simply, "Ain't God good!" He shakes his head, as if trying to figure out why the Lord would want to be so kind to him. "Yessir. God sure is good!" Then he turns and continues toward the door.

Here's a man, I think, *with no illusions.* Tired and half frozen from his long walk, he looks at a bag of canned goods and sees a truth that many people never grasp in their entire life: everything is a gift. He has a great spiritual head start on me, at least: he is completely convinced that he depends on God and not on his own efforts, while I'm still struggling with the illusion that I'm in control. I plan and organize and work hard; I use my talents and energy to get things done and then enjoy taking the credit for all of it. This poor old man with the cold hands, though, is giving me a pointed lesson in humility this morning: All of my seeming self-sufficiency is an illusion. Like him, like our monastic community, I'm totally dependent on God for everything!

We're at the door. I unlock it and am almost afraid to send him out into the blustery cold again. Sensing my reluctance, he reassures me,

"I'll be all right now. Sister gave me a dollar for the bus. I'll be home in no time. Thank you!" I unlock the door for him and push it open a crack. The icy wind rushes in, grabbing at my ankles and whipping my habit, twisting it around my knees. He turns and, from underneath the shopping bag, awkwardly offers me his hand. It's still a block of ice.

"Thank you, sir!" he says, "God bless you. And you have a good day."

"God bless you, too," I answer, "and safe home!" The heavy metal door blows closed behind him with a thud. I slide the bolt again, marveling at this old fellow. As I turn to cross the waiting room, I smile, imagining my talents and abilities filling up a big shopping bag like so many canned goods. They've been handed to me by the Lord out of sheer love. When someone says to me, "That was a good lecture tonight," or "Your French class was great today!" the old man with the icy hands will be standing beside me. We'll each be holding our bag of groceries. I'll look down at the gifts overflowing in my arms, and answer, "Yes! Ain't God good?"

And the old man will nod and agree, "Yessir, God sure is good!"

Reading and Questions for Reflection

Read 1 Corinthians 12:4-11, in which Paul assures us that each of us has been given certain gifts. List some of the gifts you believe God has given to you, and then take time to consider them one by one. Is this a gift you use a lot? Do you enjoy having it? How does this gift make you feel? Who knows that you have this gift? Do you ever thank God for it?

Describe one way you might use one of the less-used gifts you listed above.

Compliment someone on a gift of his or hers that you enjoy.

4

Searching in Prayer

Waiting With the City: Vigils

O God, hear my cry!
Listen to my prayer!
From the end of the earth I call:
My heart is faint.

I tug the hood of my choir robe down to my eyebrows to ward off the icy draft from the windows overhead, and join my brothers in the first psalm of Tuesday morning Vigils. Praying in the seat right next to me, our senior monk, Fr. Emilian, doesn't seem to notice the cold at all. Our voices spill beyond the circle of yellow light around the choir stalls to echo in the shadows at the far end of the church. At 6:15 on this winter morning, I shiver and hunker down into my hard wooden seat.

The first Christians would spend all night in praying psalms and listening to readings, watching and waiting for the Lord who was to come and deliver them. Monastic communities continue this tradition of keeping watch by celebrating the hour of Vigils in the early hours of the morning. The monks on the other side of the choir take up the next stanza,

On the rock too high for me to reach
Set me on high,
O you who have been my refuge,
My tower . . .

The horrendous blare of an air horn obliter-
ates the final verses of the psalm as a fire engine
roars up the William Street hill right beside the
church. We are on the corner of two busy streets,
so we often pray to the impromptu accompani-
ment of a siren, a rap song from some car radio,
or the rumble of a truck stopped for the light.
These sounds from the street remind us that
keeping vigil, longing and waiting for God, is a
universal experience, not just a monastic one.
Whether they realize it or not, the rest of the people of our city, who carry more than their share of
burdens, are looking for the Lord's coming, too.
They are hoping for deliverance as much as we
are—probably more. Some of them seek it in
prayer and in doing good, but others, tired of waiting, look for it in money, material things, sexual
excess, drugs, or alcohol. In any case, the whole
city is here at Vigils this morning. There is a short
pause at the end of the psalm. Then the next one,
Psalm 106, begins,

Alleluia!
O give thanks to the Lord for he is good;
For his love endures forever.
Who can tell the Lord's mighty deeds?
Who can recount all his praise?

The psalms are the heart of the Liturgy of the
Hours. It draws us into a deeper level of reality,

and we become part of the ongoing saga of salvation history. In Psalm 106 we're celebrating God's faithful presence in the events of Israel's history, but we are also experiencing that same saving love at work today in our city, our monastery, and our own lives. In this sacred dimension, our everyday existence takes on infinite meaning as part of God's unfolding, mysterious, loving plan.

> *Come to me, Lord, with your help*
> *That I may see the joy of your chosen ones*
> *And may rejoice in the gladness of your nation*
> *And share the glory of your people.*

God's love, the psalms tell us, is coursing through the city and giving it life. We can see it easily enough, say, in the bravery of the firefighters, in the hands of the doctors and nurses at University Hospital, in the hidden prayer of the cloistered Dominican nuns on Thirteenth Avenue, in Mother Teresa's Missionaries of Charity and their soup kitchen up on Sussex Avenue, and in the quiet heroism of single parents and weary grandmothers struggling to raise little children. They are all praying with us this morning.

The story of God's love is also working itself out, though, in some pretty obscure and unpleasant places as well: in the county jail up the hill, in the daycare center for AIDS babies on Orange Street, all along Elizabeth Avenue where teenagers are racing in stolen cars, in back alleys where the hungry and the homeless while away the numbing hours. You look at these places and you ask with the psalmist, "Lord, where are you? Are you really here at all?"

We continue the psalm's account of Israel's unfaithfulness,

They worshipped the idols of the nations
And these became a snare to entrap them.
They even offered their own sons
And their daughters in sacrifice to demons.

Even back then children were abused and mistreated. Vigils is no escape into a pleasant fairyland: praying the psalms leads you into the dangerous acknowledgment of how life really is. You find yourself in the presence of God, where not everything is polite and civilized and "nice."

Time after time the Lord rescued them,
But in their malice they dared to defy God
And sank low through their guilt.

The psalmist faces with the rest of us the shattering experiences and the dark times that are an inescapable part of the human condition. Sometimes I think of him as a fellow Newarker calling God to task amid the ravages of racism, drug addiction, hedonism, and despair: "Awake, O Lord! Why do you sleep?" "They prowl about the city like dogs!" "My God, my God, why have you abandoned me?" "Why, O Lord, do you cast us off forever . . . ?"

The psalms that we pray at Vigils presume, though—and this is the key—that *it is precisely in such dark and dreary places that God is at work creating new life.* In the midst of pain and despair, suddenly an unexpected newness breaks in on us, and God is once again acting in history. The story continues,

In spite of this the Lord paid heed to their distress . . .
For their sake God remembered the covenant.

It is no accident that the most solemn vigil of the year, the one that the Roman Liturgy encourages all the faithful to take part in, is the Easter Vigil on Holy Saturday. Vigils is essentially a paschal celebration, prayed with the conviction that the crucified and risen One will come again in glory in the middle of the night to finish the work of saving us.

Sometimes I can feel that newness breaking in, surprising me with the energy of the Spirit in gifts of strength, consolation, or insight. At other times, though, the psalms expose my own personal sins and shortcomings, and make me wonder how I have the nerve even to show my face at prayer. There are mornings when I bring my brokenness to Vigils and leave full of peace—but there are times, too, when I'm still waiting at the end.

Fr. Francis is finishing the last verses of Psalm 106:

O Lord, our God, save us!
Gather us from among the nations
That we may thank your holy name
And make it our glory to praise you.

I join my brothers as we recite the last stanza together in a single, resounding voice,

Blessed be the Lord, God of Israel,
For ever, from age to age.
Let all the people cry out:
"Amen! Amen! Alleluia!"

Reading and Questions for Reflection

Read Psalm 13, a prayer of someone waiting for God's help. Think of an instance when God kept you waiting for a long time. Remember the feelings you had while waiting. How did you handle it? Did you try to take things into your own hands instead of waiting?

Think of a situation in which God seems to be keeping you waiting right now. Can you say to God—and mean it—"It's okay, I can wait until you're ready"?

Singing Your Troubles: Convocation

"I want to pray for my uncle who is having an operation today."

"Lord, hear our prayer," we respond.

"Please pray for my aunt who is dying of cancer," adds another student.

"Lord, hear our prayer."

I'm squeezed between a senior and a sophomore in the second row of bleachers that line both sides of the old gym. Across the way, a bank of three rows of faces looks back at us. On the floor in between, the freshmen are sitting in neat ranks and files. We're in the middle of our daily 8:00 a.m. convocation.

Sometimes only the people sitting nearby can actually hear the student who's praying, but everyone in the gym still joins in the response.

"I ask you to pray for me and my mom. We're having a rough time getting along right now."

Hmm! Interesting! Probably explains why he's been so moody in French class lately. I'm always amazed at the private, personal things some students will pray about in front of 500 people.

"I want to lift up my girlfriend's brother who has AIDS," adds a strong voice from way across the gym. Then from just off to my left I hear a bashful freshman pray,

"Please pray for my cousin who got shot last night. He's in critical condition and they don't think he's gonna make it."

Hey, I say to myself, *this is getting depressing!* That's the way it works, though: on some days no one has anything to say out loud, but on others a flood of troubles comes pouring out.

I start thinking of the millions of people who have showed up at their jobs this morning with no way to let their co-workers know about some particular problem, worry, or family tragedy that will be weighing them down today. *I'll take our way,* I decide, *even if sometimes, like this morning, other people's troubles can start to get me down.*

The petitions end with a prayer by Fr. Matthew, who is running the service this morning. He then hands the microphone to Rev. Winstead, who is standing at the upright piano. He is a short, stocky African-American in African dress, wearing beads around his neck. When he plays a couple of chords a ripple of excitement runs through the crowded room. *"Yes!"* We've just shared a lot of pain and misery both spoken and unspoken, and we don't want to go to class feeling like this. We need to sing!

Rev. Winstead, whom the students refer to affectionately as "Rev," is pastor of a little store-front church not far away, and writes all our songs. He half whispers the first words into the microphone, *"God loves me. . . ."*

A few of us pick up the song, *". . . he never leaves me, he knows what I'm going through. Everything's gonna be all right. . . ."*

Not everyone is singing. But as more and more voices join in, the room starts to fill with music. We're just getting into that song when Rev suddenly switches to a faster one, *"Don't give up! No! Don't give up! God has never lost a battle, don't give up!"*

After weeks and months of listening to one another's worries and burdens at morning convocation, a web of trust has woven itself around us. Singing together this morning, we are lifting one another up; you can feel it happening. This must be what St. Paul had in mind when he wrote about the mystical body of Christ: not some abstract theological concept, but a community of real people sharing their joys and fears, singing and shouting together, encouraging and strengthening one other. As a monk I value quiet time and solitude as opportunities for seeking God, but I also know how much I need my community to help me in that search. Of course, community members, whether students or monks, can be aggravating at times, and the demands of the group don't always fit my immediate wants or even my needs, but in the end I know I couldn't get along without them.

Suddenly the piano shifts into a calypso beat. Without missing a note we join in the new melody, *"There's a lotta stuff goin' on in my life, but God is good, God is good. . . ."*

Dozens of us start clapping to keep time.

"Hey, hey-hey-hey, hey-hey-hey! God is good!" Some rows of students start swaying in their seats. Two or three sitting near Fr. Malachy stand up and start dancing in their places. This morning we sing the words as if we mean them, with maybe even a touch of defiance in the face of all

the troubles we've just prayed about. *"God is good!"* is the shout of an Easter community in the face of sickness, misery, and even the mystery of death itself. Off to my left, the freshman whose cousin got shot isn't singing, but is being carried along by the rest of us. That's when it really helps to be praying with a group of people who are feeling and celebrating what you are *not* able to feel at the moment: *"God is good!"*

The song ends with hearty applause. When Rev turns around and walks away from the piano, though, the whole gym breaks into a roar of complaint: we haven't had quite enough singing yet. The cheers and applause keep getting more insistent until he turns and walks slowly back to the keyboard. He leans down into the microphone and chants lightly,

"Don't let nothin' get you down!"

A few hundred voices pick up the familiar song right away, *"Don't let nothin' get you down! Don't let nothin' get you down!"*

The chorus gets louder and louder, then the shouting part:

> *Stay up! Stay up! Don't let nothin' get you down!*
> *Stay up! Stay up! Don't let nothin' get you down!*
> *Stay up! Stay up!*
> *Stay up! Stay up!*
> *Don't let nothin', Don't let nothin',*
> *Don't let nothin' . . . get . . . you . . . down!"*

This time we end with satisfied applause. Yes! That's better!

The student who is running convocation today walks to the center of the gym and raises his hand for quiet. He asks in a loud voice,

"Are there any announcements?"

Several students stand up in their places. One of them calls out,

"This afternoon the J.V. basketball team has a game here at four o'clock. We'd appreciate your support."

"Anybody who owes articles for the *Benedict News*: the deadline's next Monday," adds the next.

The body of Christ has begun another day.

Reading and Questions for Reflection

Read Matthew 11:28-30, "Come to me, all you who are weary and find life burdensome, and I will refresh you." What burdens of your own would you lift up to God right now? What about those of other people?

Do you ever ask others to pray about some specific concern that's worrying you?

"God is good, all the time!" goes a common saying in the African-American churches. Try completing the following sentence in three or four different ways: "God is good, all the time—even when _____." When you look at the answers you gave, is there any pattern that emerges? Try lifting up these cares to the Lord.

NEAR THE CROSS: GOOD FRIDAY

The liturgy can catch you off guard sometimes, surprising you with an uncomfortable moment of truth.

"Were you there when they nailed him to the tree?"

The words of the old spiritual have a special richness this afternoon at the Service of the Lord's Passion and Death. We are the usual mixture of parish and monastery: Monks in long choir robes, parishioners in African or American dress, people in business suits from the nearby courthouse and downtown office buildings, and several folks who seem to have just wandered in off the street.

The last few people in the line come up to kiss the relic of the true cross in its little gold and glass reliquary inserted into a three-foot-high wooden cross, while we sing,

"Were you there when they laid him in the tomb?"

Br. Maximilian now carries the small cross toward the apse of the church. In the six-foot-wide aisle that separates the two sets of monastic choir stalls, other servers start lifting a ten-foot-high wooden cross, standing it up in its slot in a platform. The organ intones the next hymn, one of my favorites. We start to sing:

Jesus, keep me near the cross—
There a precious fountain,
Free to all, a healing stream,
Flows from Calv'ry's mountain.

The larger-than-life brown wooden cross is now towering straight and somber, filling the whole church the way the crucified Savior's love fills our lives. Everyone is singing the chorus,

In the cross, in the cross,
Be my glory ever,
Till my raptured soul shall find
Rest beyond the river.

Many of the people are singing from deep, personal acquaintance with suffering—I can hear it in their voices. There's plenty of sin and brokenness that needs to be lifted up and nailed to the cross just in our little congregation, without even going out into the neighborhood with its crack cocaine, violence, child abuse, and HIV.

Near the cross a trembling soul,
Love and mercy found me;
There the Bright and Morning Star
Sheds its beams around me.

Suddenly the words catch in my throat: "Keep me near the cross?" I realize that I don't *want* to be near the cross. I've been there. And I don't particularly want to go again. In fact, I'd rather be as far away from suffering and death as I can get!

Once I was on crutches for two months after a knee operation and got so frustrated at my helplessness that I sat in my room in the monastery and cried. At the time that seemed like the cross. It wasn't until my brother was dying of cancer, though, that pain and grief really brought me to the foot of the cross. Even years later, just thinking about it is enough to put me there again. Believe me, I don't go there on purpose!

Near the cross! O Lamb of God,
Bring its scenes before me;
Help me walk from day to day
With its shadows o'er me.

There's a story about a church in the Midwest that was remodeling its sanctuary. The plans called for a new cross over the high altar to replace the beautiful old wooden one with its traditional image of Christ hanging in agony. The pastor asked if, rather than just destroying the old crucifix, the contractor might not be able to sell it to some other church where it could be put to good use.

The contractor paused a moment, stroking his chin.

"You know, Father, you got a problem here."

"Oh, what's that? It is a beautiful piece of art, isn't it?"

"Sure, that's not the problem. Problem is, that there's just no market for a suffering Christ."

That's *my* story—I'm not in the market for a suffering Christ this afternoon.

Near the cross I'll watch and wait,
Hoping, trusting ever,
Till I reach the promised Land
Just beyond the river.

"*Hoping, trusting . . .*" Yeah. There's the problem, all right! I sneak a glance at one woman in particular whose life has been one tragedy after another. She's singing with her whole being. I look around the church at other folks who live on food stamps, one woman whose son is in jail, a brother monk with serious medical problems. They all seem to be singing with conviction, even urgency, "*hoping, trusting ever. . . .*"

Fr. Luke, the master of ceremonies, reaches up and hangs the smaller cross with its relic onto the large cross, so that the relic in the tiny silver disk is now in the very center. While everyone in the church is gazing on it and singing of Calvary's healing power and the saving love of Jesus I start to feel more and more out of place—I still can't get myself to *ask* for a share in the cross. All I can feel this afternoon is the scary part: the image of Jesus hanging on the cross mingles with images of my brother lying in bed in the intensive care unit, hooked up to weird monitors, intravenous tubes, and an artificial breathing machine. On Calvary you've got nothing left. Nothing but trust in the Father's love: "Into your hands I commend my spirit."

> In the cross, in the cross,
> Be my glory ever,
> Till my raptured soul shall find
> Rest beyond the river.

The song comes to an end and a deep silence settles on the assembly. Everyone else seems at peace, resting at the foot of the cross. I keep my distance, though, trying to shake off the nightmare pictures from the hospital.

Maybe next Good Friday, though. Maybe by then, with the help of God's grace and the prayers of these folks, I'll find myself in the market for a suffering Christ.

Reading and Questions for Reflection

Read Matthew 27:35-50, the story of the crucifixion. Can you picture yourself among the onlookers? Where are you in the crowd? In the back? Right up front? Why did you choose this particular spot to stand? Make yourself look up at Jesus hanging on the cross. Do you want to get any closer? How do you feel?

Are you "in the market for a suffering Christ"? Think of a share of the cross that you've been given lately. Have you embraced it or have you tried to escape it? How have you felt about it— Bitter? Sad? Serene? Consider how this cross might be a source of life and blessing for you and others.

Dropping Your Shield: The Honor Code

Folks in the city live imprisoned behind window bars, deadbolts, and roll-down doors. It isn't surprising, then, that the idea of not locking your locker sounds crazier each year.

"I don't leave nothin' in my locker no more, I just carry all my stuff around with me." The teenager sounds apologetic, but convinced. He adds, as if we need an explanation, "I don't trust nobody!"

"Yeah. If they won't let us lock our lockers," adds a classmate, "nobody's gonna leave anything in them."

My homeroom group, twenty boys ranging in age from twelve to eighteen, is discussing the problem of stealing in school. As usual, a couple of students jump right away on what they see as the cause of the problem: the school's Honor Code. One of the most challenging parts of the "Covenant" that each of the students signs is the agreement that there will be no locks on lockers.

"It's a nice idea, and all, but it's old-fashioned. Things aren't like that anymore, man. This is the nineties."

In our culture, and especially in the city, "security" has become an obsession: you have to sign in at the security desk when visiting an office building downtown, you get buzzed in to retail shops, you get your Chinese take-out food through a Plexiglas barrier, and you smile up at the surveillance cameras at the local printer. We have even had to hire a security service to keep thieves from walking off with all of our school's equipment during the night.

"It doesn't make any sense. It's just dumb," continues one frustrated sophomore. From the normal city-dweller point of view, maybe he's right. But for our school family, not putting a lock on your locker is a statement to the world, a flesh-and-blood parable about a central truth in human life: there are times when it is more important to take a risk than to protect yourself from being hurt. Our attempts to shield ourselves can end up doing us more harm than good. A mindless "security-first" philosophy insidiously undermines the central Christian values of community and trust.

During the week-long freshman orientation at the start of each school year, a hand-lettered sign gets taped to the cafeteria wall: "When two African warriors meet to make peace, they don't drop their spears—they drop their shields." It's meant to get the students to think, and to forewarn the newcomers that they're going to be challenged here to a new and difficult way of looking at the world.

"There's people around here stealing," a senior complains, "and nobody does anything about it."

The Honor Code works remarkably well most of the time. Unfortunately, now and then some student starts taking advantage of his brothers, stealing money and valuables from unlocked lockers. This gets depressing for the rest of us. While students and adults are working to find the culprit, we also have to sit down in homeroom groups and encourage one another to stick with the Honor Code. Every so often we need to renew our commitment to the vision: trust is the heart of true community, and sometimes you have to leave yourself vulnerable for the sake of something more important. This is not an easy sell, especially when someone in the community is dishonest.

But, I think, *I don't have the same excuse for not trusting God!* Often I know that God's inviting me to let down my guard at prayer, but I don't want to leave myself open like that—least of all to God! It would mean running the risk of being surprised, hurt, or maybe changed for ever. My instinct for self-preservation wins out and I refuse to let the Spirit come in and take over my life.

This is the same issue that's at stake with putting locks on lockers: there comes a point at which I have to stop protecting myself and decide to take a chance. Jesus keeps inviting me to intimacy, but I show up for our encounters carrying so many shields that it would be comical if it were not so sad. One way I keep the Divine Lover at a safe distance is by doing nice things for God: I stay so busy doing the Lord's work that there's no time left for intimate, serious, self-revealing moments together. A second way I defend myself is to monopolize the conversation when I pray, filling the time with my own words, my own concerns, my own agenda. That way God never gets a word in edgewise: no challenges, no demands, no corrections.

"They should have seniors as monitors in the locker rooms."

"Yeah, or T.V. cameras!"

The "vision" is getting obscured by layers of Plexiglas and metal. The group's elected student leader sees where the discussion is going and tries to put in a word in defense of the Honor Code:

"No, man!" he objects, "This is our *school*! We can't make it like a prison! We don't want people looking over our shoulder every second!"

"It's better than having your stuff taken, isn't it?" someone challenges.

Several heads nod in agreement. In the face of the "security at any price" onslaught, the young leader backs off.

As I think of all the ways I've been protecting myself from God lately, I squirm guiltily in my seat. Giving up "security at any price" requires some courage—for all of us.

Reading and Questions for Reflection

Read Hosea 2:16, in which God says of Israel: "So I will allure her; I will lead her into the desert and speak to her heart." Imagine that God has called you to go out into the desert. Can you picture yourself there, surrounded by vast stretches of barren rock? Feel the scorching sun, and the arid air parching your throat. You have no water, no food, no protection from the elements or from wild animals. You feel completely helpless. Does it bother you to be so completely dependent on God? Do you trust that God will provide you what you need to survive?

Are there times when you take a "security-first" attitude with God? Think of one of the "shields" you use to keep God at a distance (busyness, monopolizing the conversation, distractions, and so on).

Can you pray without that shield? Imagine placing that shield on the ground and going to God in prayer defenseless, empty hands at your sides.

SPONTANEITY: MARY'S DANCE

Nye onyinye chineke, nye onyinye di mma!

From the back of the church, a woman's voice intones the offertory song in the rich liquid sound of the Ibo language, and the Nigerian refrain is quickly picked up by fifty other voices:

Nye onyinye chineke, nye onyinye di mma! "Give thanks to God; give good thanks!"

The women of St. Mary's Parish, Newark, are moving two-by-two up the center aisle in the offertory procession for Mother's Day. Not walking, exactly, but "stepping" in a stylized impromptu shuffle.

The congregation picks up the refrain, and, with the big drum marking time, the church pulses with the soul of west Africa. A woman who has stepped up to a microphone gives the "call":

Chineke kechar'anyi si ka anyi yie Ya. "After God created us, he told us to give thanks."

And everyone joins in the "response":

Nye onyinye chineke, nye onyinye di mma! "Give thanks to God; give good thanks!"

The brilliant colors of their dresses add to the joyful mood: long narrow skirts of deep blue, orange, purple, some heavy with silver thread brocade. Many of the married women are wearing high head-wraps of stiff cloth. The procession starts to look more and more like a dance, with each woman doing her own little step as she sings her way toward the altar.

I once saw a video of an ordination in Nigeria. At one point the mother of the new priest simply stands up in her place in church and begins to dance for sheer happiness. Sometimes, an African will tell you, you just *have* to dance. In spite of yourself, your arms and hips and feet just start moving and you're dancing. You don't even think about what you're doing.

I've always envied people who can express themselves that way. I never really could—at least not very well. I was always self-conscious. Even as a teenager my dancing was the result of a painful thought process, my reluctant limbs struggling to keep up with the torrent of instructions rushing from my brain.

Nye onyinye chineke, nye onyinye di mma, the call and response continues, "Give thanks to God, give good thanks!"

The procession wends its way toward the altar in the center of the church, where each woman places her envelope in the basket, is sprinkled with holy water by Fr. Philip, the pastor, and, with fingers still drawing little figures in the air, joins her sisters in the flowing, growing circle around the altar.

In the back of my mind, a thought takes hold: maybe there is a reason I can't dance. It's because I prefer things planned, controlled, and calculated.

Recently I was at a wedding reception. When the bride's elderly aunt asked me to dance with her, I smiled my usual apology,

"I'm sorry, I don't dance."

"You don't dance? What do you mean you don't dance? That's ridiculous!" The woman is half-baffled and half-incensed. "My rabbi dances," she continues, "and you can't? Why not?" Seeing that her onslaught has rocked me back on my heels for the moment, Auntie presses the attack, "So maybe you think you're too good to dance with the rest of us?"

"Well, no, ma'am. It's just that I don't— I mean I'm not—"

"Listen!" Now she's getting genuinely upset at me. "You've got no business telling people you don't dance! Just get up and dance with me, already! Come!" This is no longer an invitation or even a request—it's a showdown. Our eyes meet. We stand motionless for a few moments staring each other down. Then I blink.

"Good!" she crows. With a heavy, silent sigh I stand up and follow her onto the dance floor.

After the dance I sit down with nervous sweat soaking the small of my back, but admitting that in fact it hadn't really been all that bad. And it made her happy. A moment later, of course, the bride's mother is striding purposefully in my direction. I can guess what she wants.

Now our Mother's Day celebration continues, fifty or sixty women standing in a circle around the big, square, stone altar, stepping and waving hands in the air to celebrate God's goodness, the gift of life, and Mother's Day.

It's okay not to dance, I reassure myself, as I sit stiffly in my concelebrant's chair off in a corner of the sanctuary. *The Blessed Mother never danced, right? At least I've never heard of her doing it. Neither did her son. And God the Father certainly doesn't dance, either.* God is pure intellect, pure spirit—I remember that from the seminary. That's why I can have this nice, calm, cool relationship with the Lord. Both of us are reasonable, deliberate, and dignified.

Then, as I watch the women spontaneously singing and swaying, I realize with a start that maybe I am dead wrong; maybe *God is dancing all the time!*

That first "Let there be light!" may just have been sung out in the midst of an impulsive, whirling jig, as the Almighty cavorted with hands waving high in the air. As the days of creation went on, the Creator only grew more flamboyant: "Let there be galaxies and quasars and black holes! Let the Crab Nebula spew itself across the emptiness!" "Let there be whales and sailfish and sea otters!" "Let there be kelp and coconuts. Let there be anteaters and zebras—and camels!" And today, the Lord of Life must still be dancing in time to the blood that pulses through our arteries and the neutrinos that dart straight through our planet to come out the other side without even slowing down. God doesn't dance? The whole universe is one big dance!

The saints in the stained glass windows are glowing in the cheerful morning sunlight. It seems to me that St. Frances of Rome back there in the corner may even be swaying slightly with the drum beat as she watches the bright-colored procession.

Now, the truth has really sunk in: God is spontaneous and extravagant all the time. If I'm made in God's image, then I've buried this part of the divine likeness under protective layers of decorum and reserve.

The music stops, and Fr. Philip says a short blessing from in front of the altar. As he begins to give each woman a little gift, a voice inside the circle intones a new song, a Nigerian version of Mary's song of praise, the Magnificat:

Tobe dinwenu, mkpuru-obi nkem.

"Praise the Lord, my soul," it begins, and everyone picks up the familiar refrain:

O meere m I-he, O meere m I-he, O meere nnu-kwu ihe ebe m no. "He has done something for me, he has done something great for me."

I love this lilting little melody; it's the kind that gets in your head and sings itself for the rest of the day.

Muo m anurigo na chineke onye nzoputa m, the women chant in a haunting harmony, "My spirit rejoices in God, my savior."

They start dancing and stepping their way, a river of vivid colors, back to their seats. I join in the words to the chorus,

O meere m I-he, O meere m I-he, O meere nnu-kwu ihe ebe m no. "He has done something for me, he has done something great for me!" Some people begin a simple clap in rhythm with the words. I join in as the big drum starts to rumble in time as well. I begin to tap my left foot.

A voice from somewhere inside me asks, "Say! Would you like to dance?"

"No," I smile my usual apology, "I don't dance."

"You don't dance! That's ridiculous! I've been dancing for eternity. Out of sheer love I romanced you into existence. Now you can't loosen up and celebrate a little with me?"

O meere m I-he, O meere m I-he . . ., the mothers continue Mary's dancing song, "He has done great things for me. . . ." I picture Mary, a teenage girl, joyfully twirling and lifting her hands heavenward as she abandons herself to the divine will, her spirit rejoicing in God her Savior.

The Gospel calls us all to live life as a beautiful, spontaneous dance, making it up as we go along and responding freely to every movement of the Spirit. Am I willing to live my life that way, like the young virgin mother dancing her "Yes!" to her Lord? Can I let go of my grim, preoccupied attempts at controlling everything, my fears about making a mistake, my worries about what others might think?

The chanting finally comes to an end after the last women arrive back at their seats.

During a moment of stillness before the mass continues, I smile ruefully at my own tightness, my guarded and sober way of coming to God.

I swallow hard as I realize that my African sisters have put me on notice this morning: some time soon, the Lord is going to come up to me and invite me once again, "Say! Wanna dance?" The two of us will stand motionless for a moment, staring each other down. Will I blink?

Reading and Questions for Reflection

Read 2 Samuel 6:11-15, in which David dances before the ark of the covenant.

First imagine the "dance of the universe." Start with something you can see, maybe the leaves rustling in a tree, or some clouds moving across the sky. Picture the dance of the birds wheeling through the air, or the constant whirling of the clouds as they encircle the globe, all in time to the same music. Then the moon spinning around the earth and the earth and her sister planets around the sun. Then our solar system wheeling in a circle around the center point of the Milky Way galaxy.

Now try going the other direction, imagining the dance of the blood coursing through your arteries, its corpuscles and red cells and white cells, all dancing in time with the music. Then picture the molecules, and the atoms that make up the molecules. Then the electrons racing around the nuclei of these atoms in your body, all following the music of the same dance as the galaxies.

Now imagine yourself walking in the procession beside David. Suddenly he holds his arms over his head and starts to twirl around, dancing before the ark. Try to join him. The Lord of the Dance is inviting you to take part in the dance of the universe. How do you respond?

Go to your room, close the door, turn on some music, and dance for the Lord—if you dare!

5

Searching in the Common Life

THE COURAGE TO BELONG: THE SOCCER GAME

The November night is crisp and clear, just right for a soccer game. One of the noisy fans off to my right is waving a huge, silky flag of yellow, green, and red, while the group around him chants in Spanish: "Bo-, Bo-, Bo-, li-, li-, li-, -via, -via, -via! Bolivia! Arriba Bolivia!" I smile as I remember the six weeks I spent working at a parish in Santa Cruz, Bolivia, and the sunny soccer afternoons in Roli Aguilera Stadium. Despite the flag-waving and the Spanish cheers, though, this is Newark, New Jersey. Our high-schoolers are playing a tournament game against the Tahuichi Soccer Club from Bolivia.

I glance up into the rows of stands behind me and catch the eye of a couple of parents from school. We wave briefly and then turn back to the game.

Down on the wide field, players dash back and forth on green grass in the silver glow of the stadium lights. Most of them can make the ball go just where they want it to go and do just what they want it to do. A couple even have that sixth sense that tells them where everyone else is on the field, and can see ahead of time just how a play is going to develop. They pass the ball to what seems an empty spot on the field, and a teammate I haven't even seen appears from out of nowhere just in time.

It's the end of the soccer season. The smooth teamwork we're seeing tonight is no accident, but the result of hours and hours of exhausting practice, of time spent talking and hanging out together. From what I've heard, there were even a few struggles with one or two individuals early in the season. Some people need to be convinced that the way to be your best is to contribute your talents selflessly to the team.

A long rainbow pass slants downfield toward the sideline. One of our players sprints to get to it before the defender. At the same time, a teammate dashes straight up the center of the field toward the goal. The first player gets to the perfectly passed ball and dribbles it ahead of him without breaking stride. After two touches, he sends the ball toward the center of the field to his teammate who is still breaking up the middle. A second perfect pass! The goalie steps out to defend. Now the crowd starts to roar as we see that a third player has been streaking up the other wing. The man in the middle deflects the ball to this third teammate without even looking at him. The goalie is caught completely out of position. The white ball, glistening with the stadium lights, blurs past the goal keeper and the crowd cheers as the ball curves toward the corner of the goal. "Whack!" it slams into the crossbar and bounces harmlessly out to a defender. "Ohhh!" Everyone applauds the great play. The Bolivians clap louder, of course, because they have just survived a near-miss.

It's a joy to watch the game flow smoothly this way from one player to the next. One or two touches and you pass the ball off, moving it down the field with purpose and decisiveness. No single player is trying to impress anybody tonight; each of them is putting himself in second place to make the team work.

Benedict pictures the monastic community to be something like that—when we're at our best. "Let no one do what he finds good for himself," he advises, "but what he finds good for the other." I start to remember, uneasily, the selfish way I handled a situation last week.

The monks of Newark Abbey are playing their positions on the soccer field. I'm on left wing. Someone passes me the ball. I hitch up the black skirt of my habit with one hand and run full tilt down the field. I concentrate, staring at the ball as I dribble it ahead of me. I don't hear the shouts, "Hey, pass it! Look! Man open!" I, of course, am concentrating on doing my thing, so I don't see the brother standing alone in front of the goal waiting for me to pass the ball. By now three defenders have hemmed me in. But since my pride is at stake I have try to work my way past these guys and get a shot off. After all, some people have told me I have one of the best shots on the team. My fellow monks are shouting, "Dish it off!" "Look up!"

Finally a defender taps the ball away from me to his teammate, who sends it back the other way. My brothers shake their heads sadly as we drop back quickly on defense, hoods and scapulars flying.

A tall, blond midfielder and a short, stocky Bolivian are jumping shoulder to shoulder, each trying to head the ball in a different direction. Elbows and shoulders and hips are flying. The fans to my right shout *"¡Falta! ¡Falta!"* but the referee signals to play on—there was no foul. The ball starts its way up the far sideline.

I wonder what our lives would be like if we all worked together the way these team members do? What if there were no self-centered "stars" in families or parishes, and everyone sacrificed a little for the good of the Body of Christ? What if our love for one another in the monastery were so intense that people driving past our front door in their cars could feel it?

The crowd roars as a Bolivian player streaks down the far sideline with the ball. Three of his green-shirted teammates are charging downfield, waiting for his centering pass. There it is—the ball skims along the grass, leading a green shirt right toward the goal. It's now a footrace between our goalie and the Bolivian. Everyone in the grandstand jumps up, shouting encouragement. The goalie gets there first by an eyelash and throws himself on the ball, protecting it as if it were a newborn baby. "Yeah!" The home crowd shouts its approval.

The monastery is a reflection of the Kingdom that Jesus has in mind for all of us, where people work together selflessly, thinking of others first instead of themselves, so that we all live, work, and pray with one heart. It's a world where you sacrifice yourself out of love for your neighbor, and are always conscious of being part of a single, great unity, like this soccer team, all heading for the same goal, all helping one another to get there. It may sound unrealistic, but Jesus clearly expects all of us to spend our lives working toward just such a world.

The sharp trill of the referee's whistle carries across the field. It's the end of the first half. The score is 0-0. Everyone applauds the effort on both sides. The big silk flag starts waving again, and the chant carries on the night breeze toward downtown: "Bo-, Bo-, Bo-, li-, li-, li-, -via, -via, -via! Bolivia! Arriba Bolivia!"

Then I turn and head over toward the Bolivian cheering section to say hello, promising myself that from now on I'll keep my head up and look for a teammate as I dribble toward the goal.

Reading and Questions for Reflection

Read Philippians 2:3-5, about looking to others' interests rather than your own, in imitation of Christ. Now look at your family, your religious community, or maybe your parish. What does this community expect of you? What do you expect of yourself? Are these expectations on each side realistic and fair? If so, are they being met? Is there one aspect of belonging to that particular community that makes the most demands on your charity?

THE CLOUD OF WITNESSES: SOLEMN VOWS

When you're just starting out, you think that your vows are only between you and God. As you go along, though, you discover the truth.

"Saint John the Baptist . . ."

". . . pray for us!"

"Saint Joseph . . . "

". . . pray for us!"

"Saint Peter and Saint Paul . . ."

". . . pray for us!"

The late-morning sun is flooding into the abbey church, smudging the floor with the glowing blues and reds of the stained glass windows. Everyone is standing during the Litany of the Saints except for one young monk who is lying face down in the middle of the sanctuary. He has just professed his solemn vows as a Benedictine, publicly promising "stability and the reformation of my life and obedience according to the Rule of our Holy Father Benedict." He has just said his definitive "yes" to God's invitation, and committed himself to search for God with us in the monastery for the rest of his life. I smile as I remember my own solemn vow ceremony.

"Saint Mary Magdalene . . ."

". . . pray for us!"

"Saint Stephen and Saint Lawrence . . ."

". . . pray for us!"

"Saint Agnes . . ."

". . . pray for us!"

When I lay on the floor at the age of twenty-four with several other monks it seemed to me that it was mostly about me and God. I hardly remember who else was there at the time. But each passing year shows me more convincingly that monastic life is just as much about me and my community. Early on, I was blessed with classmates my own age who had the courage to pull me aside and point out some pretty glaring faults of mine that I didn't want to see. Then there were the older and wiser monks who had the patience and understanding to put up with my youthful brashness. By now the whole community has become essential to my journey by edifying me with their constant faithfulness to their vows, and making demands on me that move me toward patience and generosity.

Standing here as a witness for this young monk who is just beginning his life of solemn vows, I realize that I have to be a cheerleader for him the way others have been for me.

I remember jogging around the lake in Branch Brook Park as a high school student during spring track practice. I was a terrible runner, but sometimes as I dragged myself along a voice would call out, "Okay Holtzie, let's go!" or "Come on, just another half-mile!" Coming from teammates running right alongside me, they were tremendously powerful words.

"Saint Basil . . ."

". . . pray for us!"

"Saint Augustine . . ."

". . . pray for us!"

If saying your solemn "Yes!" in monastic vows means being welcomed into a community of believers who commit themselves to helping you, then this Litany of the Saints adds an even deeper dimension. As you lie there, the Church calls on the help of our ancestors in the family of faith.

"Holy Father Benedict . . . "

". . . pray for us!"

"Saint Bernard . . . "

". . . pray for us!"

"Saint Francis and St. Dominic . . . "

". . . pray for us!"

This is a celebration of the "communion of saints," connecting us here on earth with our holy brothers and sisters who have gone before. I think of the image in chapter twelve of the Letter to the Hebrews

> Therefore, since we for our part are surrounded by this cloud of witnesses, let us lay aside every encumbrance of sin which clings to us and persevere in running the race that lies ahead; let us keep our eyes fixed on Jesus, who inspires and perfects our faith.

Here is the image of a great grandstand packed with saintly ancestors rooting for us and cheering us on, encouraging us to "run with perseverance." The people in the stands all have run this race themselves and have earned their place in the ranks of those who encourage the rest of us.

I start to think of some of our own particular ancestors in the faith who made vows in this very church and lived their lives in this monastery: I remember Fr. Luke Mooseburger, who kept riding his bicycle around the city well past the age of ninety until the abbot made him stop. I think of the stories of Fr. Peter Petz and his wooden leg, and Fr. Damien Smith who went about teaching others who had to learn—as he himself had had to learn—to speak without a larynx. These stories, passed on from one generation to the next, are an important part of a monastery's identity and history. Our community, then, has its own litany, our list of special cheerleaders:

"Father Eugene . . . "

". . . pray for us!"

"Brother Denis . . . "

". . . pray for us!"

"Father Celestine . . . "

". . . pray for us!"

Will anyone look back at my story one day, I ask myself, *and be able to find encouragement and inspiration in it?*

"Saint Ignatius of Loyola . . . "

". . . pray for us!"

"Saint Vincent De Paul . . . "

". . . pray for us!"

"Saint John Bosco . . . "

". . . pray for us!"

We all hope to move on into the grandstand some day and join the cloud of witnesses watching, cheering, interceding for others.

"Saint Scholastica . . . "

". . . pray for us!"

"Saint Catherine of Siena . . . "

". . . pray for us!"

"Saint Teresa of Avila . . . "

". . . pray for us!"

But until we get to the finish line, we run buoyed up by the community of ancestors urging us on, and encouraged by the voices of brothers and sisters running beside us.

"All holy men and women . . . "

". . . pray for us!"

Reading and Questions for Reflection

Reread Hebrews 12:1-2, already quoted in the chapter. Imagine yourself running a race on a track in front of a huge grandstand packed with your ancestors in the faith. Some are your favorite saints, others are the people who handed the faith on to someone centuries ago, making it possible for you to receive the gift of faith from someone yourself. Some are deceased family members or friends. As you start to get tired and begin to slow down, you start to recognize some familiar voices cheering you on and encouraging you. Let each voice evoke a name and a face. Listen to the different things each one is saying to you.

Write out a litany of your "ancestors" in the faith, and recite it with the refrain, "Pray for us!"

PEACE UNDER PRESSURE: THE FRENCH QUIZ

"But you never told us we were having a quiz today!" the indignant student protests loudly.

"Please sit down and take the test!" I whisper fiercely. "Everyone else is working already." I give him my best glowering stare until he retreats in sullen silence. "Thank you!" I whisper to the back of his head as he shuffles to his desk in the front row.

"I still ain't takin' no quiz!" he mutters, just loudly enough to make sure I'll hear, as he throws himself noisily into the seat. I fight to keep calm.

A little stained glass window over the door of the monastery proclaims the Latin motto *"Pax,"* "Peace." Many people seem to take this as sort of an advertisement that claims the monastery is a sea of calm and serenity. It's true that the cloister is a very quiet place: we keep strict night silence after 9:00 p.m. and there are no televisions or CD players blaring. But this outward peacefulness, while very important, is not what the motto refers to.

Peace is not the starting point of the monastic life, but rather its goal. Peace doesn't just happen: we work at it full time. Benedict assumes, in fact, that there will be plenty of pressures working against the peace of the monks.

The *Holy Rule*, especially toward the end, lists all sorts of irksome things that will disturb one's inner calm: a monk is commanded by the abbot "to do impossible things"; a brother loses his temper and strikes one of the boys or another monk; the poverty of the monastery means that the monks have to do the heavy, menial work of harvesting themselves; or the prior of the monastery starts to think of himself as a second abbot. Benedict, then, certainly doesn't expect a "peaceful" life in the sense of an undisturbed, stress-free existence behind the cloister wall. Just the opposite, in fact: he expects us to learn the knack of finding what someone has aptly called *"peace under pressure."*

The sophomore is now slouched in his seat, staring straight ahead, while everyone else is busy with the French quiz. He is deliberately, as we say in our neighborhood, "working my nerves." I decide to ignore him for now, and walk to the back of the classroom checking the other students' work.

Monks are just people, and we bring to community life our personality traits (good and bad), our feelings and sensitivities, our personal histories, and our brokenness. So every day the monastery offers plenty of challenges: being misunderstood, being irked by people's idiosyncrasies, knowing that I could do a much better job than that monk is doing, wondering why the Abbot lets that monk get away with murder.

Finding peace under pressure is not just a monastic undertaking, of course. Psalm 34 is meant for all of the faithful, "Let peace be your aim." Benedict's methods of finding peace, based on scripture and centuries of experience, are simple practices from which every Christian can profit.

First, at the center of Benedict's theology is one of the best helps to finding peace under pressure: humility. If I am willing to admit that I am not God, that I don't need to be in control of everything and everyone, and am, in fact, just an imperfect creature like everyone else, then when things don't go exactly as I want, I'm much less likely to feel upset.

Second, Benedict stresses the attitude of service and "solicitude" toward others. If my first concern when I encounter someone is always to try to be of service, then when someone is unkind or unfair to me, I'm able to see that person first as a brother or sister in need of help, rather than as someone who is violating my rights.

He still hasn't started taking the quiz. In fact, he has now opened his Biology book. *So,* hisses a little voice inside me, *he wants to pick a fight with me, eh?* I feel my blood pressure rising as I stalk slowly back up the aisle toward him. *Let's just see who wins this one!*

A third help to "peace under pressure" is the habit of continuous prayer. A monastic tries to keep up a constant dialogue with the Lord no matter where he or she is. If I'm in the habit of thanking God for simple little pleasures, and offering up little sufferings, then when a really stressful situation comes along, my automatic reflex will be to hand it over to the Lord, to let it be God's problem and not mine.

I'm standing beside him now, staring down at his Biology book. He's obviously not reading it, but is dangling it in front of me like bait on a hook. For a moment I contemplate grabbing the book and smacking him over the head with it.

As a monk you spend a lot of time each day in *lectio divina,* the slow, meditative dwelling over scripture, waiting for it to speak to you about your own life. You ask yourself, "What does this verse mean for me here and now in terms of my daily living?" As you get in the habit of asking this same question all during the day about all sorts of events and situations whether good or bad, it becomes a fourth way of staying peaceful under pressure. Instead of fighting it immediately, you find yourself asking out of habit the same questions you ask during daily *lectio:* "What does this mean for me? What is the Lord trying to teach me here?"

Of course, you don't always manage to take the peaceful way out. Sometimes, for whatever reason, you lose your temper with someone, or get all churned up inside because work is piling up too fast, or everything's going wrong at once. But then you can console yourself with the idea that peace under pressure is, after all, a *goal.* Tomorrow will bring lots of chances to work on it again, and so will the next day, and the next.

As I stand over this angry student's desk, I take a deep breath and clear my throat.

Reading and Questions for Reflection
Read Romans 14:17-19; taking special note of the phrase "make it your aim to work for peace." When and where do you find yourself having to find "peace under pressure?" What are some of the forces that work against peace in your life?

Lift up one specific situation to the "God of Peace" (2 Thes. 3:16), asking for the gift of peace under pressure. Then ask the Lord what you're supposed to learn from this situation.

CLOSING THE DISTANCE:
HALE-BOPP

I pick my way carefully up the last tiny, steep steps, remembering to keep my head down as I duck through the low doorway onto the monastery's roof. Six of us are hoping to get our first look at the Hale-Bopp comet, which has been putting on quite a show the past two days. Now that I'm safely out on the gravel-covered roof, I raise my head and gasp in astonishment.

"Oh! Look at that!" I exclaim.

Right in front of me, just over an apartment house to the northeast, Hale-Bopp is shining like a perfect silver tadpole swimming through the clear night sky.

"That's incredible!" someone says.

"Beautiful!" whispers another.

We step over to the short, fat telescope that Fr. Mark has set up ahead of time.

"Take a good look, fellas!" one of the monks says as we gather around. "I read in the paper that the last time this comet came by was over 4,000 years ago, and it won't be back for 2,400."

I stoop and look down into the eyepiece with one eye. The silent, mysterious visitor glows brightly against a background of dozens of faint, silvery flecks. It's streaking away from the sun at thousands of miles an hour, but in the powerful telescope it seems strangely still, like a specimen frozen on a microscope slide.

"How far away is it right now, Mark?" somebody asks.

"Actually, it's pretty close," he answers. "Only about 120 million miles away!"

"I don't know, but that sounds pretty far to me!" quips another voice.

I straighten up and step aside so Fr. Theodore can look. The modern buildings of downtown Newark glow off to my right. To my left looms the modern courthouse, behind it the county jail, and beside them a sea of neat, new brick townhouses that spills down the hillside from University Hospital. Turning my back on Hale-Bopp, I can see the twelve-story housing projects, the kind that one poet called "filing cabinets of human lives."

To be honest, the icy blob of Hale-Bopp doesn't really look much different in the telescope, so Fr. Mark offers to move on to something more interesting. "Okay," he says, "who wants to see a galaxy?" He swings the telescope to the right of the comet, until it points to a spot high above the Newark Museum. After peering down into the eyepiece and tweaking the fine-focus knobs, he steps back and invites Br. Francis to take a peek.

"So now what is this I'm looking at?" he asks politely, squinting into the lens.

"See the bright oval in the center?" Fr. Mark asks.

"Oh, yeah! What's that?"

"That's the Andromeda Galaxy. It's our nearest neighbor galaxy."

"Wow! That's pretty!"

After a few moments, he steps away and motions for me to have a look. I take off my glasses, bend over the tiny lens again, and squint down into a black pool. This time there's a miniature oval jewel floating among scores of tiny stars.

"Wow! That's incredible!" I mumble, dazzled by its beauty and magnificence. Even a microscopic galaxy is somehow awesome to look at. "How far away is it?" I whisper.

"Oh, somewhere over two million light years," comes the answer. That means that the light that's hitting my eye right now has been traveling 186,000 miles a second for more than two million years.

"Huh!" I mumble noncommittally, not knowing quite what to say under the circumstances. After a minute or two of staring across hundreds of millions of empty miles I offer, "Anybody else want a look?"

As I straighten up and roll my head around a couple of times to get the stiffness out of my neck, I think, *If our nearest neighbor galaxy is over two million light years away, no wonder some people think that God must be that far away, too!* It figures that the God who made the galaxies and strewed them across the universe like this is probably light years off in some distant corner, with no interest in what's happening on our tiny planet, and with no more effect on our lives than an explosion inside the Andromeda Galaxy.

Actually, I admit to myself, *there are times when I wouldn't mind if God really were like that: safely distant, unconcerned, and undemanding.*

The God of the Bible, though, is a personal God, a God who took flesh and became one of us. This tremendous Lover keeps inviting me to deeper intimacy in prayer, in sacrament, and in selfless love for my brothers in the monastery and the kids in school. The "Hound of Heaven" keeps chasing me down the corridors of time, while I, running away, pretend to be searching for God.

"The Milky Way is a spiral galaxy, too. It looks something like the Andromeda, but it's a lot smaller." Fr. Mark is finishing his commentary as Fr. Augustine takes a turn at the eyepiece. "Andromeda is around 160,000 light years across."

160,000 light years across! These distances are starting to make me nervous. The whole idea of the Christian calling is to close the distances that divide us from one another. In the monastery you work constantly at overcoming things that separate you and God, you and your superior, you and your brothers or sisters. You can't retreat to the safe, impersonal distances of deep space by replacing intimacy in your life with, say, efficiency or effectiveness at work, or mastery of some skill. That would be to quit the quest for God.

If we are frightened by the vast, overwhelming distances of space, we as Christians ought to be just as frightened by the distances we put between ourselves and God, and the spaces that we carefully arrange between ourselves and our sisters and brothers.

I glance up at the glowing pinprick of the Andromeda galaxy, surprised that I can actually see it without a telescope. But 2,000,000 light years is still far away. I need the comfort of something closer. I turn toward the Hale-Bopp comet, a mere 120 million miles off. Still too far. In a space between two buildings of Newark's skyline, the Empire State Building glows fourteen miles off in Manhattan. That's better! My eye is drawn to the right, to Newark's Ironbound neighborhood where I was born, just a mile from here. Even better! Then I look around me on the roof at my brothers Mark, Ted, Ed, Augustine, and Fran, all staring up at the stars and chatting quietly. We know each other inside out, and have shared each other's fears and foibles, tragedies and victories for years. Tonight, they seem closer than ever.

Reading and Questions for Reflection

Read Ephesians 2:19-22, where Paul reminds us that we are no longer strangers and aliens, but members of God's household. Can you think of specific individuals in your family, community, or circle of friends who are "distant" from you emotionally or psychologically? Is this distance their choice? Yours? Do you want to go about closing this distance, or just let it take its course? Is it possible that you are being called by the gospel to close that distance?

All Together:
Freshman Backpacking

"What's the worst thing that can happen to a backpacking team when you're in the woods?" the teenage instructor asks his class.

"Getting lost?" answers a timid voice from the back of the classroom. The desks are arranged by teams: four circles of eight students each.

"Somebody gets hurt real bad?" suggests another. He's wearing the white baseball cap of a captain. The logo on the front shows that he's the elected captain of the "Hawks."

It's the first day of the Freshman Backpacking Project. Each May all the freshmen—divided into teams of eight—hike fifty-three hilly miles of the Appalachian Trail, between High Point and the Delaware Water Gap.

More ideas start popping up:

"Rain?" "Bears?" "You get bit by a rattlesnake or something?"

"Nope!" The junior who is running the session and who is going to be in charge of these four groups when they're on the Trail, cuts the list short. "Listen to me. Write this in your notebooks, 'cause we're gonna expect you to know the right answer from now on. The most important rule on the Trail is *'Stay together.'* The worst thing that can happen to you in the woods is that you get separated from your team."

Thirty ballpoint pens start scribbling dutifully in thirty notebooks.

"Your teams," the junior continues, glancing down at a typed page in his loose-leaf binder, "will always have plenty of food, water purification tablets, and protection from weather. As a group you can be lost for days and have nothing to worry about. But when you're in the woods *by yourself,* all sorts of things can happen." He looks up and starts ad libbing: "Can anybody think of bad stuff that can happen to you if you're in the woods all alone?"

"You can get hurt and have no one around to help you."

"Okay, that's true. Anything else?"

"You can lose your way, and then run out of food or water."

"Sure!" the teenage teacher agrees, "People have gotten lost and wandered for days in the mountains, right in New Jersey, near where we're gonna be hiking. The most important rule on the Trail is *'Stay together!'*"

All the freshmen are listening hard. Most of them are from the city, and will be thoroughly out of their element in the woods, where street survival skills are completely useless.

I can imagine what's going through their heads. Older students, who have already done the hike, have spent the winter scaring the freshmen with visions of haunted swamps and quicksand pits, and tales of man-eating bears, and rattlesnakes that like to crawl into warm sleeping bags.

Stay together is certainly the most important safety lesson we teach during the five-week project. It is worrisome enough for the adults in charge to watch for an overdue team as darkness falls, but imagine the feeling in your stomach if an eight-man group comes filing out of the woods with only seven hikers!

The Freshman Backpacking Project is really about facing challenges and getting along as a member of a group—the camping part is secondary. From the first day of the three-week training period at school, the freshmen do everything as teams. If one member forgets his pen, his whole group marches single file back to his locker with him to get it. If one member is late for school, the other seven run laps with him. From one point of view, it doesn't seem "fair" to make someone pay for another's mistake, but it prepares the students for the realities of the hike. The team will walk only as fast as their slowest member. When one of them has to stop to fix his broken backpack, everybody else will stop with him. When someone is in a bad mood, the whole team is going to feel it.

American culture, with its stress on self-reliance and rugged individualism, misleads us into believing that in the "real world" the most important thing is to be independent and able to fend for yourself. The truth is, though, that in the real world we're all interconnected, interdependent. We rely on others to grow our food, make our clothes, and provide our electricity. Our lives are affected for good or ill by the actions of people we don't even know and will never meet. At work or in school, we need to rely on people to collaborate with us in groups and teams. Learning how to be interdependent, though, is harder than learning to just do things for yourself—and teaching teenage boys how to work together is much harder than teaching them how to compete against one other.

"Staying together" is actually a gospel ideal. Over and over, Christ challenges us to be a community. The Acts of the Apostles, in fact, is the story of the first Christians wrestling with this challenge. In his first letter to the Corinthians Paul scolds them for their selfishness. He then sets out the image of the mystical body of Christ: each person is most fully herself or himself precisely to the extent that she or he is united to the body of Christ.

In his Letter to the Galatians Paul says, "Carry one another's burdens, and so you will fulfill the law of Christ." An image jumps into my memory from a hike many years ago, in the days before our trained first-aiders and CB radios. One student has gotten terrible leg cramps and can't walk. So the strongest member of his team has picked him up and is carrying him piggy-back up the side of a mountain to the campsite, while the other members somehow manage to lug the two extra backpacks.

St. Benedict in his *Rule* calls for the monks to pray together, eat together, read and work together. We are to observe the Lenten fast not as individuals but "all together," as a community. Chapter 72, in which he summarizes so beautifully what the monastic life is all about, ends, "Let them prefer nothing whatever to Christ, and may he bring us *all together* to everlasting life." Even the goal of salvation itself, which seems so individual and personal, is one we are to reach "all together." My brothers have certainly had to carry me more than once on our monastic journey, and I can only hope that I've done my share of carrying, too.

I'm startled by the noise of chairs scraping on the floor. The freshmen are filing out of the room in their groups, on their way to "team challenges" down on the ball field.

"Captain of the Hawks," the instructor warns sternly, "make sure your team is walking together!"

Reading and Questions for Reflection

Read John 14:20-23, where Jesus prays at the last supper, "that they may all be one." Reflect on a particular community you are called to live in (family, parish, religious house, and so on). When is the "Stay together!" rule hardest for you in that community? How often do you act as a rugged individualist? Think of some specific behavior or attitude of yours that may be working against the unity of that community.

Which is easier for you: asking someone to "carry your backpack" for you awhile when you need help, or offering to help someone carry theirs? Look for the opportunity to do the one you find less easy!

6

The End of the Journey

HOPE: ADVENT ON MARKET STREET

The December wind lashes my face as I turn onto Market Street for the last leg of my long walk. These days it's already almost dark at four o'clock. As I lean into the wind and head up the street, I'm struck by the fact that although Christmas is only ten days away, there are hardly any holiday decorations to be seen. An anemic string of lights blinks in front of the Chinese take-out place, and a few strands of tinsel do their best to liven up the hardware store window. On each of the light poles the city has put up a colorful banner displaying a generic holiday symbol: a candle, a trumpet, a snowflake, a wreath. The candle banner reminds me that this evening the monks will gather in the refectory before supper for the Abbot to bless the third of the four candles on our family advent wreath.

The rich readings and rituals of Advent speak right to the heart of the Christian life and the monastic project: waiting in joyful hope. Like our Israelite ancestors, we are a people of the promise, being drawn forward through history not by the sight of God's face here and now, but by the vision of a mysterious, glorious future. St. Augustine in his *Confessions* puts it, "We are made for you, O God, and our soul is restless until it rests in you." Hoping in a future is part of being human. Hope has inspired people throughout history to deeds of heroism, sacrifice, and greatness.

The sad saga of humanity, however, is that as the hoping stretches on and on, and our expectations are repeatedly frustrated, we often lose our nerve. Impatient and depressed because our life seems to have no meaning, we turn to cheap substitutes—money, prestige, possessions. Somehow, we trust, they will give life some semblance of meaning, and more important, some immediate satisfaction.

"Fr. Al?" It's the mother of one of my French students.

"Mrs. Winslowe? It's good to see you," I respond, shaking her hand. "How's everything?" Then I notice her daughter, a kindergarten student in St. Mary's school, holding her mother's hand. "Hi! How are you this afternoon?" I ask the little girl. But she's being shy today. So I wink at her and turn back to her mother.

"Well, anyway," I continue, "how are you doing?"

"Oh, fine! I'm just so busy with shopping and what-not, trying to get ready for Christmas."

"I know what you mean! It can get crazy this time of year."

"You got that right! I'll be glad when it's all over!" she admits.

"Well, listen, I've got to get back up the hill. Nice seeing you. And you too, Alicia."

"Alicia, say g'bye to Father." She crinkles her fingers in a bashful wave, which I return with a smile. Then I turn back into the wind.

I'll be glad when it's over. How many people, if they were honest, would say the same thing?

The hectic, pre-Christmas shopping season is probably our culture's most powerful example of misplaced hope. The deep hunger and longing inside each of us draws us to the shopping malls by the millions as merchants count down the days left before Christmas. Evan Christians, who are supposed to know better, get caught up in consumerism's blind rush after false hopes and empty promises, scurrying around faster and faster to finish their shopping. Year after year we go through the exhausting ritual of preparing for "the holidays," waiting for a payoff that never comes. The fact that every year we get disappointed doesn't seem to deter us, though. By next year we'll have forgotten the fiasco and join one more time in the hectic rush, determined that this time it'll work. "Hope," someone said, "springs eternal. . . ."

Yet when you picture life in the center of our cities, "hope" is about the last word that comes to mind. Not even holiday shopping time seems to help. If the pre-Christmas season is often shallow and materialistic in the suburban malls, it's even worse for the poor of our cities for whom even the hollow promises of the consumer religion are out of reach. That's why celebrating Advent downtown is so crucial: folks who live here seem to need its message of promise more than most people.

The insistent booming of a rap song throbs from a speaker in front of a clothing shop, assaulting everyone, young and old, with a stream of angry obscenities—not exactly Bing Crosby singing "Silver Bells." I hurry to get past without being too obvious about it.

In our neighborhood, where there is little hope of escaping, and no sense of looking forward to a brighter future, the holidays provoke a wave of frustration, anger, and violence. That's why one of the surest signs of the holidays downtown is the presence of more policemen on the streets—along with an increase in assaults and domestic disputes.

Monks, even more than other Christians, have the chance to lead lives that clearly point past the material preoccupations of the world to a realm visible only to the eyes of faith, a kingdom of mustard seeds and buried grains of wheat. Our way of living ought to make us a sign of hope to our neighbors, a sign that says "Be patient! There's more to the Kingdom than what you can see right here and now—and we're betting our lives on it!" Here in the center of the city, this witness of quiet, patient hope is our most subtle, but also our most important gift to our neighbors. Another candle banner flutters unnoticed overhead. *"May this candle,"* says tonight's prayer over the advent wreath, *"reminds us of Jesus the light of the world as we call upon him whose coming we prepare for and await."* As I climb up the last two blocks of our hill, I look at the school buildings and the church tower. I'm suddenly humbled by the thought that God has called us to be keepers of the vision in the middle of the city's bustle, busyness, and holiday frustrations, like advent candles quietly reflecting the promise of another and better world.

The bells start to sing out from our church tower, riding the cold wind down the hill, inviting everyone to Vespers. As I quicken my pace up the windy hill, I start humming tonight's advent hymn:

> *O Come, divine Messiah,*
> *The world in darkness waits the day*
> *When hope shall sing its triumph*
> *And sadness flee away.*

Reading and Questions for Reflection

Read Philippians 4:4-9, were St. Paul encourages the Christian community to live in love because "the Lord is near." For Paul, belief in the future coming of Christ is not just an intellectual idea, but a call to live in a certain way: to be charitable, joyful, peaceful, and persevering. Look at your personal priorities, and ask yourself whether they reflect your belief that there is more to life than the passing promises of this world. Do you ever respond to the plight of victims of urban poverty or world hunger so that they can have some sense of hope for the future? How might you share with others the gift of hope that you have received?

DIMINISHMENT: CHUCK TAYLORS

One morning some years ago, back when we could all fit into the cafeteria for convocation, I came to realize that I still had a long way to go before I could start pointing a finger at teenagers.

"What?" A junior who has been sleeping his way through morning convocation in the row in front of me is now suddenly wide awake. "No way! He's gotta be kidding, man!"

"Chucks? I ain't wearing no Chucks!" The sophomore sitting next to me grumbles under his breath. All around, a rebellious rumble of complaints is welling up among the three hundred students seated in neat rows in the cafeteria.

The headmaster has just dropped a bombshell: from now on, the only kind of sneakers that students will be allowed to wear for gym class will be Converse All-Stars, the "Chuck Taylor" model, with black tops. Known popularly as "Chucks," they sell for about twenty dollars a pair.

"Well, that's what's gonna happen in September," the headmaster continues. "The Executive Committee of the Parents' Organization suggested it a while ago, and we announced it to your parents at the meeting last night. They all clapped. They thought it was a great idea."

"Yeah, but they don't have to wear them!" quips a comedian in the back. Everybody laughs, but there are still grumbled protests in the air.

A few of the young faces around me show disbelief, disgust, and disappointment. For a lot of our students, your sneakers are a way of expressing who you are, a statement about your deep-down self. The more you spend on them, of course, the better. (In fact, if your mother has the good sense to buy basketball shoes at a discount store, you save face by simply telling everybody you paid a higher price.)

"How come? Why can't we just wear whatever sneakers we want?" comes a respectful but pointed challenge from a senior.

"Because you guys are dopey enough to pay $125 for a pair of basketball shoes," answers the headmaster, "and then you leave them sitting around somewhere. And after you lose them, your parents are dopey enough to go out and buy you another pair. It's ridiculous. If you have that kind of money to waste on sneakers, then I'm going to raise the tuition!"

The dissent is now reduced to tooth-sucking and head-shaking. Fr. Ed has just won another battle in the never-ending war against the Street.

Besides being easier on parents' pocketbooks, the move to have everybody wear "Chucks" is teaching something important: with all the needy people in our city (not to mention the Third World), a Christian should want to think hard before spending $125 for a pair of gym shoes.

I can almost feel the sense of loss in the crowded room. It makes me feel kind of smug.

Look at these kids! I grumble to myself. *They put so much stock in material things. They need to have some idea about living frugally and simply, like us monks. Take me, for instance. I'm not attached to anything. There's nothing that I have that I couldn't let go of easily.*

Suddenly a vivid memory comes back to me. I'm rolling on the frozen grass clutching my knee and shouting in pain through tightly clenched teeth. A circle of worried faces is staring down at me, causing a time-out in the student-faculty touch-football game. Just when I think I'm going to pass out from the pain, my kneecap seems to readjust itself and the agony subsides. At the age of thirty-eight I have just said good-bye forever to the anterior cruciate ligament in my left knee.

As I hop to the locker room, leaning on two faculty members, I realize vaguely that I'm leaving something important behind me on that field: the ideal of perpetual youthfulness. I don't like the feeling, and don't let go very gracefully. Eleven weeks on crutches, however, will give me plenty of time to get used to the idea.

"Any more questions about sneakers for gym class?" asks the headmaster. A brief, stony silence.

I start to think of other things that I have had to say good-bye to. Every time I get my hair cut, for example, Joe the barber tells me in his Italian accent, "Hey, Padre Alberto, you know, I can remember when your hair was black like coal. Now it's all gray." Entries in my journal during the early 1970s often start out something like: "Feb. 19, 1974. 12:45 a.m. Today was a busy day. . . ." It was after midnight and I was sitting down to write in my journal! Nowadays I start wilting before nine o'clock.

"What if you already bought some other kind of sneakers for gym?"

"I can't stop you from wearing them at home," Fr. Ed answers, "but you're not wearing them in gym class."

Everybody knows that life is a process of constant diminishment. As our bodies and our various abilities and powers start to weaken and fade, some of us accept this and make it part of our story, but others go kicking and screaming—yet diminished just the same.

For Christians, this natural process has a deeply spiritual dimension: it is a way of identifying with Christ who emptied himself for us, taking on human weakness, even to his passion and death on the cross. As limitations start to close in on me, I can see them as my share in the diminishment that Jesus suffered. They are God's way of getting me right where I need to be—vulnerable and open to divine grace. My losses are a way of warming me up for that one final act of detachment when I'll be bereft of everything. They are unmistakable signs that the Bridegroom I'm waiting for will be coming some time, and I had better be ready to go out and meet him.

Monks practice poverty and asceticism, and meditate often on the cross and on the Lord's coming at the end of time. We ought to be able to show the rest of the world how to do this right, how to suffer little diminishments gracefully. But even though I try to do this "getting older" business with as much good humor as possible, deep down inside I still don't like letting go of these things—it's like someone taking away my Air Jordans and making me wear Chucks instead.

"So in September," the headmaster concludes, rubbing a little salt in the wound, "the Physical Education department will have sneaks on sale here." Their long faces are eloquent—they don't like the idea at all.

Hang in there, guys. I know the feeling.

Reading and Questions for Reflection

Read Philippians 2:5-8, about Jesus emptying himself to become one of us. Have you ever experienced being "emptied" against your will, or had something taken away from you that you were attached to? What did it feel like? What did God teach you by the experience?

Is there some way in which you are being called to voluntarily let go of some privilege or power that is rightly yours? Ask yourself if this very moment might just be one of those times when God is giving you a special grace—the ability to let go right now.

Traveling Light:
The Appalachian Trail

I stick my thumbs under the shoulder straps of my backpack and shrug the weight up a little higher on my shoulders. The eight students hiking single file in front of me have been chattering non-stop. They seem to have a lot more energy than I do this morning. I'm already aching in muscles that I didn't know I had, and the blister on my left foot is starting to bother me—and it's only ten o'clock!

This is the third day of the fifty-three-mile freshman backpacking hike along the Appalachian Trail in the mountains of northern New Jersey. We're due to finish up in the Delaware Water Gap in another two days.

"Oh, sweat!" a voice shouts from the front of the line. The students collect in a circle to stare at something on the ground. I bring up the rear and peek between two backpacks to see the great attraction. All I can make out is an ordinary groundhog hole about ten inches across. I don't know why that should be such a big deal.

"Damn! Imagine the size of the rat that lives in that hole?" someone marvels nervously, his voice a mixture of wonder and fear. I stifle a laugh. The teacher in me wants to correct him, but the child in me says to keep my mouth shut.

"Man, I ain't waitin' around here to see," a second voice chimes in.

"Let's get goin'!" adds another, uneasily, stepping backward, his eyes riveted on the ominous opening in the ground.

The city slickers hustle off down the trail and plunge into a green tunnel of mountain laurel and dogwoods. Nobody dares look back.

Little incidents like this are only part of what makes the hike so enjoyable. Early this morning I stood with a group of hikers at the edge of a cliff and watched in awed silence as, far below us, a hawk soared above the cottony fluff of clouds that filled the valley. Yesterday there was the top of Sunrise Mountain, with its welcome breeze and breathtaking view. Monday it was a noisy brook that chuckled and sloshed invitingly alongside the trail.

The Appalachian Trail is not always a smooth path. At times it is nothing more than a series of white blazes on trees and stones stretching across a field of sharp, punishing rocks. At other times it's a stairway of boulders, with steps two feet high. This is why I want to keep my pack as light as possible.

I've picked up little hints from avid backpackers, people who make it a point of honor never to carry even a single ounce more than they have to. You can, for example, cut the handle of your toothbrush down to two inches, carry only a quarter of a bar of soap, half a towel, and a quarter of a roll of toilet paper (we call it "all-purpose paper") with the useless cardboard core removed. You have two sets of shirts and socks: you wear one set while the other, which you've washed in a stream, gets pinned on the outside of your pack to dry in the sun as you hike. The demands of traveling light force you to decide what you really need and what you can get along without.

All Christians are called to be seekers, to journey toward the kingdom. In the Prologue to his *Rule*, Benedict uses several images of journeying, such as, "If we wish to dwell in the tent of this kingdom, we will never arrive unless we run there by doing good deeds." The trick is to "travel light" through life, carrying only the most necessary baggage. Jesus tells his seventy-two disciples as they set out, "On the journey do not carry a walking stick nor a traveling bag. Do not wear sandals on your feet." He wants them to rely on God's providence alone to see them through.

Monks are supposed to be specialists in this sort of travel, like veteran backpackers who refuse to carry one ounce more than they need to. We promise through our vows to choose carefully what we put on our backs, so as not to weigh ourselves down with over-concern about the things the world deems essential: pleasure, possessions, power, and popularity. The way we live can remind our brothers and sisters outside the monastery that they can travel carrying much less weight than they might think.

We get to the top of a long, steep hill. My heart is pounding and my breath coming in quiet rasps.

"Okay, guys," the thirteen-year-old captain shouts, "hold up. Let's take a break!" I try not to look too relieved as I sink heavily onto a boulder and let it take the weight of the pack off my shoulders. There is a light breeze rippling through the pale green haze of spring buds and tiny leaves. Beneath the backpack, my wet shirt is clammy against my skin. As I look around and enjoy the lovely play of the gray rocks of the ridge against the blue sky, I also sneak a quick look at the freshmen around me. Some of them are finally starting to look tired, too, thank God!

One of my favorite backpacking stories is the one about Terrence. Halfway into his hike, Terrence spots a beautiful piece of granite about the size of a cantaloupe. He's so taken with its pretty, sparkling colors that he decides to bring it home with him. So he picks it up and starts carrying it. Down a steep ridge. Up the next mountain. After twenty minutes the new weight is making his hand ache. He switches hands a few times as he lugs his prize across a wide meadow in the blazing sun. At the next rest break he takes a long, hard look at his rock: somehow it's not as pretty as it seemed at first. Back on the trail again, the rock keeps getting heavier and heavier and Terrence's face longer and longer. He starts to picture himself hauling his homely treasure for another three days. After a few more minutes, when he thinks no one is watching, he just casually lets it slip from his hand. It rolls under a laurel bush by the side of the trail a mile and a half from where he picked it up. So much for pretty rocks!

We each have a light pack when we start out on life's way, but are always tempted to add unnecessary junk to it as we go. The most obvious example of this is our way of grabbing on to material possessions. Even a monk with a vow of poverty has to be careful that his room doesn't start getting stuffed with all sorts of junk. There is a more subtle and therefore more dangerous kind of baggage, however—the invisible kind. Some people, for example, collect grievances, holding on to them doggedly for months, even years. Others accumulate destructive emotions such as jealousy or resentment, and stagger through life bent and exhausted under the extra weight. My own tendency is to load my pack with worries. Now, of course I know that they don't accomplish anything and just use up energy, but that hasn't stopped me from hauling quite an impressive number of them up and down the hills of life over the years.

The monastic tradition offers some ways of keeping your pack from getting heavier once you're on the road. One is frequent, careful, and honest introspective prayer. This is a way of inspecting your own backpack to discover things that are keeping you from loving, that are just slowing you down on your quest. When you dare to look into your pack, you will gradually come to see the useless items for what they are, and you'll have a chance to toss them aside, like Terrence did with that piece of granite.

Benedict suggests a second way of keeping your pack light: let someone else see what you're carrying. By humbly disclosing to a superior, a spiritual director, or a soul friend "the movements of our heart," we can avoid collecting there all sorts of useless and destructive baggage.

"Okay, let's get going!"

The captain is moving us out already? I thought we were supposed to rest! I struggle to my feet with a resentful grunt and settle the pack on my back, trying to let the waistband take more of the weight this time. After a couple of these trips, as I've gotten a little wiser, my backpack, which used to weigh over thirty pounds, has gotten lighter.

I hope one day I'll be able to say the same for my spiritual luggage, too. Seeking God is that much easier the fewer favorite burdens I carry in my heart.

We're picking our way down a steep, rocky hillside. At the bottom is the campsite where we'll stop for a lunch break. At that point we'll be exactly halfway to the Delaware Water Gap. And I'll celebrate by taking this pack off completely for a little while—I think I'm still carrying some extra weight!

Reading and Questions for Reflection

Read Matthew 11:28-30, in which Jesus calls to those who are "weary and find life burdensome." In what way does that description fit you?

Open up your life's backpack and look at the burdens you find there. Sort them into two piles: ones that are there because you choose to hold on to them, and those which someone else or some circumstance has put there. Now go back to the first pile and choose one that you're ready to leave behind.

THE BANQUET GUEST: OTIS

The long buffet tables are loaded with huge bowls of salad, piles of rolls, and trays of seafood. There is a line of guests in front of the barbecued chicken, and another at the dessert table. Everything is bathed with a golden glow as the sun filters in through the canvas sides of the giant, white tent.

No one seems to mind that it's so crowded in here. In fact, the close quarters add to the festive atmosphere of the dedication of our new gymnasium.

Men in suits and ties, women in pretty dresses, religious sisters, and black-robed monks are all standing around in knots of conversation, or eating at the dozens of round tables. Teenage students stand in threes and fours listening to alumni from the 1940s tell tall tales.

"Oops! Excuse me!" I blurt out as I bump into someone who has just turned away from the buffet with a plate loaded with shrimp.

"Oh, hi, Father!" he greets me. "Hey, this is great, man, you know?"

It's Otis, a man in his late twenties, who lives on the street. His clothes, as usual, are filthy and worn. His wiry hair is matted and badly in need of a brushing.

"Otis! How are you doing?" I answer with a wide smile. "Yeah, this sure is great! Glad you're here!" I really *am* glad, too.

Some of our other guests peek discreetly at this unsavory character in their midst. I can't blame them—at first glance you might think that he's completely out of place at this nice affair. Sometimes there's a voice inside my own head that can huff, "What's a character like *that* doing here?" This is my little judge. I picture him dressed in a black judicial robe and wielding a gavel which he pounds on anything nearby as he pronounces sentence on the endless stream of people who don't live up to his high standards.

"Listen, I got to go check out the chicken, okay? See you later." Otis melts back into the crowd, eating shrimp as fast as he can.

I think about Jesus warning against judging your neighbor. It's simple: If you want to be accepted at the messianic banquet, then you have to accept others now. In fact, if you can't stand "them" (whoever the particular "them" is) in this present life, you are warned that there will be lots of "them" seated at the heavenly banquet with the rest of us. So you might want start looking at "them" differently now, or else the heavenly banquet table will be hell for you because you're sitting next to one of "them."

The monastic fathers and mothers in the desert used to caution against judging others, but for another reason. For them, humility was at the center of the Christian life, and the best way to stay humble was to identify with the sinner instead of condemning him or her. You can keep in close touch with your own human frailty by identifying constantly with the sinner: today it's that person who's sinning, tomorrow it'll be me. I keep trying to follow their advice, and let the humbled, broken sinner who's inside of me head off the judge before his gavel comes down. The results so far have been rather mixed.

Otis looks right at home, though, enjoying the excitement and the crowd. And why not? Our friends, relatives, and alumni, our students and their parents, are a wonderfully diverse group. We are African-Americans, Latinos, and European-Americans, Christians, Muslims, and Jews.

I think of Isaiah's image of the Heavenly Banquet, the Banquet of the Kingdom that will mark the end of time.

> On this mountain, for all peoples,
> Yahweh Sabaoth is preparing
> A banquet of rich food, a banquet of fine wines,
> Of succulent food, of well-strained wines.
> On this mountain, he has destroyed
> The veil which used to veil all peoples,
> The pall enveloping all nations;
> He has destroyed death forever.
> Lord Yahweh has wiped away the tears from every
>   cheek. . . .

Otis makes our party complete. Wandering among the other guests in his dirty wash pants and grimy shirt, he is drawing us all into that parable of Jesus, where the king sends his servants out into the byways to invite beggars to the wedding feast.

The image of the Heavenly Banquet is, in fact, one of Jesus' favorite ways of talking about "the Kingdom that is not of this world." Every Christian lives in the shadow of the end-time, knowing that the present age is passing away. Monastic men and women, however, witness to this belief more intensely by a life that says clearly: "There's more to life than what the world offers!" The monastery, where we own everything in common and live a frugal lifestyle, points beyond the mad passion for acquiring things. Our life of obedience and humility points past the world of power and popularity to a different Kingdom. Everything we do whispers, "Psst! There's more! There's so much more!"

If the life of the cloister points beyond itself to the day when all people will feast at the table in the Kingdom, then this afternoon's buffet is just the kind of party that we Benedictines ought to be throwing!

As I walk around greeting people, I keep trying to catch another glimpse of Otis, and I'm not sure why. He's just a guy who stops by now and then looking for food or soap or a few dollars, and then disappears for weeks at a time. He survives on the streets by his wits: stretching the truth here, working an angle there, and not trusting anybody. Still, there is just something about him today that I can't quite put my finger on. . . . Then it hits me, and the little judge inside of me blushes deep red: *To God, I must look exactly like Otis!* Don't I always try to "run games" and work angles with the Lord, instead of just trusting? Don't I often stretch the truth in conversations with God, and try to fast-talk my way out of spiritual challenges rather than face them? Don't I sometimes wander off somewhere without saying good-bye, instead of staying single-minded in my commitment to God? Otis has brought me face-to-face with my real self, and has reminded me that I don't measure up at all.

One day, though, it'll be my turn to go to the banquet. There'll be this big white tent crowded with people of every age and race and language and nation, and tables heaped with rich food and bottles of fine wine. And I will have to show up just as I am, unkempt in my faults and my weaknesses, my insincerity and my faintheartedness, an obviously unworthy guest at the party. I breathe a silent prayer that I'll feel as comfortable at that feast as Otis does here this afternoon.

He has worked his way over to the table where they're serving the barbecued chicken. Seeing another familiar monk, he waves his plastic fork at him in greeting. His mouth still half full, he calls:

"Yo! Br. Tom! Great party, huh?"

Reading and Questions for Reflection

Read Luke 16:19-31, the parable of the rich man and the beggar Lazarus. Picture your life as a banquet table where you're seated with various friends, family, and acquaintances. You're having a wonderful time enjoying the company and the good food. Now look away from the table, searching the dark corners of the room for a Lazarus that might be lying there unnoticed. Who are the people that you are most likely not to notice, who might be "invisible" to you the way the beggar was to the rich man? Think of one of these "invisible people" and ask God how you might reach out to him or her.

THE NEW JERUSALEM:
EASTER VIGIL

St. John is on to something in the last chapter of the book of Revelation. He says that in the end, we're all going to wind up in the city. The victorious Lamb, the conquering Christ, the River of Life, all of these will appear on the last day not in a lush garden or a majestic forest, not in a misty valley or on a snowy peak, but in a beautiful city—downtown!

The damp night breeze whips across the ball field from Springfield Avenue, bringing with it the familiar grumble of traffic noises. A hand reaches out to protect the tiny flame the Abbot has just struck. Stooping low, he touches the lighted taper to a small heap of sticks and kindling piled in the middle of the brick-paved plaza behind the school and monastery. The wood slowly crackles to life, spewing ragged flames into the breeze and sending flickering shadows dancing across the wide circle of monks and a few dozen other worshippers. The white vestments of the ministers turn a dull orange.

The big white Prudential building, the old Bamberger's department store, and the Midatlantic building look on silently in the dark from a few blocks away. A stone's throw to the north, the stately Essex County Courthouse stares at us with wide window eyes. Behind me loom the ghostly shadows of our school buildings. Using the silvery glow of the security lamp mounted on the wall of the gym, Abbot Melvin reads a prayer from the book:

> *Father, we share in the light of your glory through your Son, the Light of the World. Make this fire holy, and inflame us with new hope.*

The heat from the fire brushes my face and my hands. I smile as I stare into the bright, joyful flames and feel that familiar rock-solid certainty deep inside. It comes back like this each year when we celebrate the Easter Vigil. At this moment I'm as sure of this as I am of anything: *in the end, Good is going to win.*

The prayer continues,

> *Purify our minds by this Easter celebration, and bring us one day to the feast of eternal light. We ask this through Christ our Lord. Amen.*

Fr. Theodore holds the new five-foot Easter candle while the Abbot, tracing over the cross that is painted on it, says:

> *Christ yesterday and today,*
> *The beginning and the end,*
> *Alpha and Omega;*
> *All time belongs to him*
> *And all the ages;*
> *To him be glory and power,*
> *Through every age and forever. Amen.*

"I am the Alpha and the Omega, the beginning and the end." There it is, Christ's promise in the book of Revelation that through all the upheavals of history, through all the dizzying ups and downs of the city, through all the problems and sorrows of my own life, he will remain Master and Lord of the Universe. Sooner or later he will overcome the world's darkness once and for all.

The Abbot lights the tall candle, and Fr. Theodore, lifting it up, starts carrying it across the parking lot, towards William Street. We all follow in procession while its fragile flame flickers against a cloudy sky made lavender by the lights of downtown. A motorcycle spatters and roars a few blocks away; a jet rumbles into Newark Airport. The sounds of the city seem magnified by our silence.

We walk out through the gate of the parking lot, turn right, and follow the candle up the steep William Street hill. Lay people in winter coats, black-robed monks, white-robed priests and servers slowly and reverently climb the sidewalk alongside the abbey church. A car driving up the hill beside us slows down for a look at this curious collection of hooded figures in black robes and white albs. I wonder what the car's passengers are thinking?

Walking on the city streets in a liturgical procession in the middle of the night is an important sign to the world that the Kingdom is already present and is breaking in on us. It's a reminder to all of us that the city is at the center of the Christian vision of the end time. John says in the book of Revelation:

*I saw the holy city, the new Jerusalem, coming
down out of heaven from God, prepared as a bride
dressed for her husband. Then I heard a loud voice
call from the throne, "Look, here God lives among
human beings. He will make his home among
them; they will be his people, and he will be their
God, God-with-them. He will wipe away all tears
from their eyes; there will be no more death, and
no more mourning or sadness or pain."*

If God wants to live among people, then where
better to go than a city? What better place to start
wiping tears away?

An ambulance wails somewhere in the distance.

One of the signs of the end-time is the unsettling
reversal of merely human expectations: the mighty
get knocked from their thrones and the lowly are
lifted up; the hungry are filled and the rich go hungry. The world's system of values is turned upside
down: money, military might, and moral self-right-
eousness count for nothing, and the kingdom goes
instead to the poor and repentant.

Another sign of the messianic age is the bringing together of all the peoples of the earth. In the
very last chapter of Isaiah, the Lord proclaims, "I
come to gather the nations of every language; they
shall come and see my glory." In the second chapter of the same book is this beautiful canticle,

In the days to come,
The mountain of the Lord's house shall be estab-
     lished as the highest mountain,
and raised above the hills.
All nations shall stream toward it; many peoples
     shall come and say:
"Come, let us climb the Lord's mountain,
to the house of the God of Jacob,

That he may instruct us in his ways
and we may walk in his paths."

In those days people will no longer hate their brothers and sisters for having skin that is a different color from their own. We won't feel threatened by neighbors who were born in a different country, nor despise folks for speaking with a foreign accent. As one great family we will all stream to our home downtown and crowd into the city on top of the hill.

St. John writes as if the New Jerusalem were already here, and the victory already won. Although we may be living in it, the Holy City is not yet complete. There is clearly a lot more work to be done. And for this God needs our hearts and hands. Each of us is called to build the city of God through a life of love, of humble openness toward others, and generosity toward the poor and the needy.

Traditional monastic theology often speaks of the monastery—optimistically, I suppose—as a head start on heaven, a foretaste and model of the kingdom of light and peace. As monastics, then, one of our tasks is to spread the vision of the New Jerusalem to our brothers and sisters, encouraging them, by our life of community, poverty, and prayer, to take up the gospel challenge to transform creation. Building the City of God is a pretty intimidating task for all of us, whether inside or outside of the monastery. We can all use the encouragement of John's image:

In the Spirit, he carried me to the top of a very high
mountain, and showed me Jerusalem, the holy
city, coming down out of heaven from God. It had

all the glory of God and glittered like some precious jewel of crystal clear diamond.

I walk slowly, with my eyes cast downward, keeping half an eye out for broken bottles. There's an empty Sprite can and a couple of Burger King wrappers in the gutter.

Do we have the eyes St. John had, to see the New Jerusalem breaking in around us? Do we have the will to work at building it in our own lives, in our homes and monasteries, in our parishes and cities, in our nation, and our world?

At the top of the hill now we turn right, and the procession starts to wind its way toward the church's open doorway.

Standing at the entrance Fr. Theodore, holding the lighted candle up high, sings into the cavernous dark, "Light of Christ!"

The rest of us, standing out on the sidewalk, reply, "Thanks be to God!"

As I start up the steps I smile at the vision of our city's people all living in harmony and peace as one united family, and King Boulevard paved with diamonds. Still a little work to be done here!

Inside the church we pass the flame from the single paschal candle, each of us lighting our own little taper. As the white walls of the church start to glow with the steady brightness of a hundred tiny lights I pray an Easter prayer for Downtown Monks:

Lord, give our little abbey on the hill the eyes to see your new creation breaking in on us right here in Newark. Grant us the courage to work for the day when the vision of peace will be a reality and all downtown will glow with the glory of your eternal light. Amen.

Reading and Questions for Reflection

Read Revelation 21:1-5, the description of the new Jerusalem coming down from heaven. Are there any signs that the new Jerusalem has been breaking into your life recently? What new things has God been doing in your life? Are there any new things that you know are about to happen (a change of address, a new job, a birth, or perhaps a death)? How do you feel about this newness? Do you resist it or welcome it?

Identify two or three of your gifts that could help to build the City of God on earth (the Kingdom of peace, justice, kindness). What specific course of action could you take that would make use of one or more of your gifts for this purpose?

Epilogue

I'm so glad you were able to spend some time with us. Let me walk with you back to Broad and Market. . . .

The cars in front of the monastery? They belong to parents waiting for their sons to finish up at sports practices or study hall. Later tonight, there will be even more cars—there's a lecture at seven, part of a series on racism that the abbey is sponsoring.

Yes, the kids at the bus stop are ours. The buses are less crowded now: most of the commuters are already gone. In another hour it'll be just us and our neighbors.

Let's turn down Market Street now. That's Otis waiting for the light in front of Burger King. Haven't seen him around for a while, but he looks like he's okay.

Look over there, across the street in front of the furniture store. See that Latino couple with their two boys and teenage daughter? I wonder if that's Maritza. She'd be about that age by now.

If you glance into the video arcade as we go by, you may spot William, killing time. He's probably hoping that maybe darkness won't fall tonight—even though he knows that it will.

Well, here we are: the corner of Market and Broad. That distinguished-looking old gentleman standing by the newsstand looks a lot like my friend from the food pantry, the one with the icy hands. Wonder how he is.

All these folks belong to our extended monastic family: our neighbors, the students of our schools and their parents, our alumni, faculty, and coaches, the Sisters of St. Joseph who work with us, our benefactors and lay Benedictine Oblates, the parishioners of St. Mary's, people who come for the lectures or Sunday Vespers, and those who stop by for noonday mass or five o'clock community Eucharist, as well as the dozens of local youngsters who play "Brick City Soccer" on our fields on Saturdays. Recently our family has grown even more with the help of the Internet—people have started visiting us at all hours at our web site, <http:www.newarkabbey.org>.

Looks like we have just a few minutes of daylight left now. You know, most of the city around us seals itself up after dark. The stores slam their steel roll-down doors and shrivel behind them. Even these tall glass towers that are reflecting the orange sunset will close up and shrink, too.

Funny, but the abbey does just the opposite. Did you know that at night a monastery's walls dissolve and extend outward? The boundaries of our peaceable kingdom, for instance, stretch themselves way up the hill to embrace the jail, the new townhouses, the hospital, the little storefront churches, and the thousands of people asleep in their beds, from right here out into the suburbs. The monastery expands down the hill, too, enfolding the office buildings and stores, the railroad station and the Hispanic and Portuguese neighborhood, reaching right on over through Jersey City to New York. It's hard to explain, but at night, it becomes a little easier to see that we all belong to one community.

Well, I know you've got to get going. God bless. Thanks again for visiting with us, and don't forget to pray for us downtown monks.

The Author

A native of Newark, Fr. Albert Holtz joined the monastery at the age of twenty, and is now Director of Novices and Choirmaster at Newark Abbey. At St. Benedict's Prep School, he served for twenty-five years as Director of Curriculum, founded the school's Gospel Choir, and currently serves as a teacher of French.

Fr. Albert enjoys long walks around downtown Newark, but has also worn out a pair of hiking boots on the forest trails of northern New Jersey sharing with students his Benedictine love of mountains.